11 Secrets Successful People Know About Goal Setting

A SCIENCE-BASED GUIDE THAT TURNS GOALS
INTO REALITY

Kevin E. Kruse
New York Times Bestselling Author

www.KevinKruse.com

11 Secrets Successful People Know About Goal Setting / Kevin Kruse. —1st ed.

Achieve Anything You Want, Without Delay, Derailing, or Procrastinating

What if your goals for wealth, health, and love went from impossible to inevitable?

Based on scientific research and interviews with hundreds of self-made millionaires, entrepreneurs, sales professionals, athletes, and straight-A students, New York Times bestselling author Kevin Kruse teaches you:

- How to break through your "safe zone" by reprogramming your mind

- How to turn dreams into goals with the JFK Man on the Moon Formula

- How to achieve goals faster than before with FFLs

- How to sustain resolve with three levers of commitment

- How to unlock bigger goals by leveling-up your [learning

- How to eliminate bad habits with the Friction Formula

- How to defeat self-sabotage with Time Travel

- QUIZ: The 'Impossible to Inevitable' Assessment

FREE GIFT #1
GOAL SETTING WORKSHEET

"Dream Achiever Goal Setting Template"

As a thank you for buying this book, I'm offering you a free gift! This fillable worksheet is the template I've used to build multi-million-dollar companies, to write bestselling books, and to maximize my health and fitness.

Tap Here or Scan QR Code Below
to Grab FREE Goal Setting Worksheet!

FREE GIFT #2
FREE AUDIOBOOK

If you're a fan of audiobooks, we have exciting news for you.
For a limited time, you can download the audiobook version of
TITLE for FREE (usually priced at $12.95) by simply signing up
for a 30-day free trial of Audible!
(Note: You must be a new user of Audible)

Tap Here or Scan QR Code Below
to Grab FREE Audiobook from Audible!

Contents

WARNING: This Book Might Ruin Your Life

A dozen years ago, on my patio. It's a chilly night; the fire pit warms me. I sit with an Old Fashioned in my left hand and this book manuscript in my right. I sip the Bulleit bourbon cocktail, pause, and toss the stack of papers into the fire. A year's worth of writing crackles and turns into smoke.

I originally wrote this book over a decade ago and promptly dragged it into the recycle bin on my computer and burned the paper copy. Not because I thought it was a bad book but because I had a change of heart during the year it took to write it; I feared what it might do to readers' lives. I feared for your life.

It sounds dramatic, but I really believe goal setting is like magic on Earth. But just like powerful magic in movies and books, it can be used for good or for harm. Think Gollum's ring in The Hobbit, think Peter Parker's powers in Spider-Man, or all the magical spells that go awry in Harry Potter.

From my own experiences, I credit goal setting with busting me out of a lower middle-class background and becoming a self-made millionaire at age 30. I credit goals with enabling me to start and sell several multi-million-dollar companies after the first one. I set a clear goal to become a New York Times bestselling author, and within two years, poof! It happened.

But I also think my goals contributed to a bad marriage that ultimately ended in divorce. For many years I wasn't a very present or fun father. My goals continue to have the unintended consequence of taking a toll on my health.

Less dramatic, but perhaps more important, as I achieved more and more "success" in life, I began to struggle with a lack of significance. I began to see goal setting as a way to stay focused on "doing," which is a great way to avoid feelings and just being.

When you do goal setting "right," you are, by definition, telling yourself that you are incomplete, you need more, and you are not enough. Not so good for mental health.

When my children were very small, I'd guide them through a vision-board exercise each New Year's Eve. Now I'm horrified by that idea. Why can't they just play, have fun, create art, chase flow states, and ultimately, just focus on being happy today?

I remember reading a blog or an Instagram post from some super successful entrepreneur who showed his family on vacation in Hawaii. He was standing in front of a flip chart—an actual flip chart!—writing out the agenda for the day. He boasted of his vacation efficiency, optimizing events and "fun" for his family. I saw that picture and imagined what it must be like to be his kids starting each morning as if it were a business meeting and setting smartphone alarms to go off when it was time to move to the next activity. I think that guy's a jerk.

So why does this book exist now? What brought it back from the ash heap (literal and digital)?

I literally spent a decade thinking about the two sides of goals. Their power and the peril.

And in that time, I interviewed hundreds of successful people for my LEADx Leadership Show podcast. And I interviewed many people about living a more balanced life, including Zen monks, psychologists, and resilience experts.

And some, like pastor Mark Batterson, gave me specific ways to make goals less dangerous.

And my friend and fellow author Dorie Clark, over dinner in Miami, explained that I had a unique opportunity to write two books in one. Explain how I tapped the power of goal setting in my early career, and then write or rewrite how I view goals from my perch of wisdom today.

Well, for better or worse, thank God for backup copies recovered on a hard drive. I rescued the original manuscript and updated it with a new final chapter that shares my new thoughts about managing the downside risks associated with goal setting.

This is a book of spells. How you will cast them is up to you.

Just remember, with great power comes great responsibility.

Kevin E. Kruse
Philadelphia, PA
www.KevinKruse.com

"So, Goals Made You A Millionaire?"

When my kids were younger, sometimes they'd ask if we were rich or if we had a million dollars, and I'd always answer the same way:

We're rich in love, and that's all that matters.

And then they'd roll their eyes.

"Did you make a million dollars from goal setting? How many millions?"

I always squirm a little when a reader or someone in the audience at one of my talks asks the "M Question" or some variation on it. My Dad raised me to be humble, and of course, it isn't polite to talk about things like salary or net worth or politics or religion. Obviously, that was before social media when talking about all that stuff became a sport.

Fun Fact

There are 62,500,000 millionaires and
2,668 billionaires in the world.
(Source: Credit Suisse Global Wealth Report 2021)

But I also understand the curiosity. I'd be skeptical about taking health and fitness advice from someone who weighs 400 pounds with cholesterol over 300. I'm not sure I'd trust marriage advice from someone who's been divorced four times or worse, never been married at all.

But goal setting isn't just about money or getting rich. It can be applied in a lot of ways. So let me answer the question this way...

I was born lower-middle class, and at age 22—after the failure of my first business—I had $15,000 of credit card debt, a car without air conditioning, and a cardboard box full of clothes. That's it. I went from living in my one-room office and taking showers at the local YMCA to sleeping on my friend's couch. (Thanks, Mike!)

Since then, I have shaken my head at how many times my reality ended up matching my goals:

- I had a goal to be a millionaire by age 30; I sold my first company for $1.75 million when I was 30 years old to a company called Raymond Karsan Associates.
- In 2003 I started and built a company using aggressive quarterly business goals; I hit a $12 million annual run rate in just four years and sold the company to Huntsworth Health in 2007.
- In 2010, I made a goal to become a *New York Times* bestselling author; in 2011, I co-authored the book, *We*, with Rudy Karsan, and it hit the *New York Times*, *Wall Street Journal*, and *USA Today* bestseller lists.
- As a way to "give back," I created a goal to build 10 libraries for disadvantaged kids in Asia; I've done 17 libraries so far in China and Vietnam through the non-profit group The Library Project.
- When my three kids were toddlers, I created a goal to have them go off to college physically and mentally healthy, drug-free, and not pregnant; Amanda graduated from Hofstra in 2020, Natalie graduated from Fordham in 2022, and Owen just finished his first year at Clemson. So far, so good.

I share all of that not to impress you but to impress *upon you* how important goal setting has been in my own life.

And while goal setting has been a major factor in any success I've had thus far, I'd also say that **time mastery** and **social capital** are just as important. (I haven't written a book on social capital just yet, but you can learn time mastery from my book, *15 Secrets Successful People Know About Time Management.)*

So, while the title of the book is about achieving success through goal setting, remember, success isn't just about money. It isn't just about career achievements. It's a powerful force you can use to improve your health, relationships, and really anything!

Your dreams are your dreams, and I'm confident that becoming a goal setting guru will be a big step in making them come true. But be careful because often they come at a price.

—*Kevin Kruse*

The Einstein of Goal Setting

How One Obscure Scientist Proved Goals Work Like Magic

"WHATEVER YOU DO, OR DREAM YOU CAN, BEGIN IT. BOLDNESS HAS A GENIUS AND POWER AND MAGIC IN IT." —JOHANN GOETHE

"REALITY IS WRONG. DREAMS ARE FOR REAL." —TUPAC SHAKUR

---

goal

The end toward which effort is directed.

What if you could summon Aladdin but weren't limited to only three wishes?

Wouldn't you love to be able to pull wealth from a cauldron to whip up a love potion on demand? Or how about being able to summon Abracadabra abs?

What I'm about to say is weird. But it's the first thing you really need to understand. Here it goes...

Goals are the closest thing we have to magic on Earth.

There I said it.

Learning how to set goals is like learning how to cast magic spells.

I Don't Believe In 'The Secret'

Let me be clear. I'm not some new age, crystal-wearing, firewalking, power-of-intention-chanting, granola-dude. (OK, I do like granola. But watch out—those calories will sneak up on you.)

I believe "thoughts are things," which I learned from the book *Think and Grow Rich*, but I don't believe in *The Secret*. No law of attraction made me rich. I'm pretty sure the Universe doesn't care about my bank account, love life, or body-fat percentage. I am a skeptic when it comes to manifesting results out of thin air.

And yet, as I mentioned in the preface, over and over again, my reality ends up matching my goal setting. My income, my wealth, my books, my health, my cars, and my kids...all ended up really closely matching my goals.

And when they don't, I can look back and usually see where I strayed off the proven path that you'll learn later in this book.

Setting goals correctly, and unlocking their power, is still not understood by most people. But scientists agree that goals have tremendous power.

How A Poor Kid From Canada Used Goal Setting To Become Hollywood's Biggest Comedian

Fifteen years old, so poor that he's living out of a van with his parents and brother just outside Toronto. Goes to high school in the day and works eight hours as a janitor at night. From a young age, he learned how to entertain his depressed mother and bond with his father, who always wanted to be a comedian but who took the safe route and became an accountant.

James was unable to continue the brutal schedule and dropped out of high school at age 16. He continued working as a janitor as he honed his comedy routines. He thought that if it doesn't work out, I could always try to get a good job at the Domasco Steel Mill.

Eventually, James moved to Hollywood, where he knew the action was. Broke and without any work or leads, he decided to write himself a check for $10,000,000. In the comment section, he wrote, "for acting services rendered." And he post-dated it Thanksgiving 1995.

He described what happened next in an interview with Oprah:

> *I put it in my wallet, and it deteriorated. And then, just before Thanksgiving 1995, I found out I was going to make ten million dollars for Dumb & Dumber. I put that check in the casket with my father because it was our dream together.*

The most important part of Jim Carrey's story is that he was quick to add, "You can't just visualize and go eat a sandwich. You have to do the work."

Scientists Prove the Power of Goals

If I were to ask, "Who was the genius who discovered the theory of relativity $(E=MC^2)$ and has a crazy mustache?" You'd answer, "Albert Einstein!"

Well, did you know there is an Albert Einstein of goal setting?

Yep, his name is Edwin Locke.

Edwin Locke, Ph.D., is a psychologist and the Dean's Professor of Motivation at the University of Maryland. For over 50 years, Dr. Locke has researched goals and achievements and has published over 300 scholarly articles, chapters, and books on the topic.

I once wrote Dr. Locke a letter—almost twenty years ago—and he mailed me an uncorrected proof copy of his book, *A Theory of Goal Setting & Task Performance.* 413 pages of his academic research with his corrections scribbled in black ink!

This tome sits on my bookshelf as sort of a goal setting souvenir—or even talisman—to remind me of Locke and the huge mountain of evidence that shows if you want to improve, to achieve, to have a better life, goal setting is the closest thing we have to magic on Earth.

Even back in 1990, Dr. Locke, Dr. Gary Latham, and other researchers had already completed over 400 laboratory and field experiments that examined over 40,000 men and women worldwide, looking at over 88 different types of goals.

Over and over again, Locke and other goal researchers confirmed that people who set goals outperform those who merely "try their best." The range of findings is quite interesting and amusing:

- Goal setting rugby players increase their number of ball carries
- Goal setting basketball players grab more rebounds and have fewer turnovers
- Goal setting health-seekers decrease their resting heart rates
- Goal setting savers pile up more cash for retirement
- Goal setting negotiators get better deals
- Goal setting spouses have more "marital intimacy"

And one of the more unusual findings, in a 1975 study by Dr. Gary Latham, it was shown that lumberjacks produced more cords of wood when they participated in goal setting.

Takeaway

In dozens and dozens of experiments—regardless of who was being studied or what it was they wanted to improve—goal setting was consistently shown to achieve better results.

POWER TWEETS FOR MOTIVATION

"Unlock your full potential with goal setting! Clear targets pave the way to success, as every small step takes you closer to the life you envision. Dream big, plan wisely, and watch your progress soar! #GoalSetting #ChaseYourDreams"

"Remember that every goal starts with a single step! Break down your dreams into manageable tasks and celebrate each accomplishment. Success is within reach when you stay focused and motivated! #PowerOfGoals #KeepMovingForward"

"Aim high, set goals, and never lose sight of your aspirations! The power of goal setting is immense, fueling growth, ambition, and determination. Make your dreams a reality today! #GoalsMatter #DreamsToReality"

"The sky's the limit when you set ambitious goals! By constantly challenging yourself and pushing boundaries, you unlock unlimited possibilities. Embrace the journey and let your goals inspire greatness! #LimitlessPotential #GoalDriven"

"Time is precious, so use it wisely! Establish clear, measurable goals and commit to making progress every day. The power of goal setting transforms your time into a purposeful journey toward success. #TimeManagement #GoalsForSuccess"

SECRET #1

Goals are the best way to get what you want—
and always better than just "trying your best."

HOW MIGHT YOU APPLY THIS?

- **NETWORK MARKETING PROFESSIONAL**: What goal do you really want to achieve? Your goal could be anything from just getting your own product paid for, to having 100 people in your downline or becoming "a jewel."
- **SALES PROFESSIONAL**: Is your goal your commission target or something beyond? Want to be #1 on the leaderboard? Want to open up the giant Acme account? Want to be promoted to sales manager?
- **MANAGER / LEADER**: Consider your annual and quarterly objectives. Do they align with your manager's objectives? Do they align with your organization's strategic objectives? How do your KPIs relate to your goal?

- **CREATIVE ENTREPRENEUR**: Is your goal to get free products from sponsors? Or to attract 100,000 followers? Or to get $5,000 per sponsored post?
- **INDIVIDUAL HEALTH**: Health can mean different things. Could goals improve your mental health? Do physical fitness goals pertain to just how you look or also to your cholesterol levels?
- **ATHLETE**: Depending on where you are in your career, goals can help you to make the varsity team, get into a D1 program, become a starter, make the NBA, or become an All-Star.
- **SPOUSE OR PARENT**: Most people don't think of setting goals for their relationships. But why not? They work for everything. What kind of relationship do you want to have with your kids in the year ahead? With your spouse? With your parents?
- **STUDENT**: Many successful students set goals for their overall GPA. Consider goals for each individual class too. If your overall goal is a 3.5 on a 4.0 grading scale, perhaps a lower goal is acceptable for your more challenging classes.

Self-Coaching Or Book Club Questions

1. Have you set goals in the past? Why or why not?
2. Does the research on goal setting make you believe even more in the power of goals? Why or why not?
3. How can you make sure the goals you set are aligned with your values?

From Safe to Superhero

The 4 Ways Goals Reprogram Your Mind

"HOW WE HANDLE OUR FEARS WILL DETERMINE WHERE WE GO WITH THE REST OF OUR LIVES. TO EXPERIENCE ADVENTURE OR TO BE LIMITED BY THE FEAR OF IT." — JUDY BLUME

"THE KEY TO CHANGE... IS TO LET GO OF FEAR." — ROSEANNE CASH

---

safe·ty

The condition of being safe from undergoing or causing hurt, injury, or loss.

What If You Woke Up Tomorrow Without Any Fear?

I'm here to tell you it's not your fault.

Can't seem to get out of bed at 5:00 AM to jog? It's not your fault.

Can't seem to swap chocolate cake for a piece of fruit? It's not your fault.

Can't muster the courage to ask for a raise? It's not your fault.

Can't muster the courage to ask Hunter out on a date? It's not your fault.

Whose fault, is it?

It's your brain's fault. And you are not your brain. (And if you really want to get all Zen about it, you are not your thoughts. But unpacking that is for another book.)

Our Brains Are Wired For Safety, Not Success Or Happiness

In order to honestly believe in the magic of goal setting, you should understand how goals work. I've sometimes wondered, "Why do we need goals at all? How come humans don't automatically give it our all and get what we want?"

The reality is that we all have a two-million-year-old cave dweller brain that is designed to keep us safe. The cave dweller's brain is wired to keep us safe in a world filled with threats.

Why get up early and exert energy when we can maximize safety by lying down in our cave for as long as possible?

Why pass up a high-calorie snack when we don't know when we are going to find our next meal? And let's get as fat as possible when we can so we can survive the winter.

Why confront the alpha cave dweller with a request or new idea when they might get mad and throw us out of the tribe? Best to keep our heads down and not make eye contact!

And most importantly, when we do leave our cave to hunt and gather, let's be hyper-vigilant. We want to freak out (i.e., fight, flee, or freeze) with every sound we hear, lest it be a saber-toothed tiger. We want to go into stress overload if we venture into a new part of the tundra because we might get lost, and dangers are unknown.

KEY POINT

Our brains are great at keeping us alive but not so good for truly living.

And the psychological impact runs far deeper.
- We fear loss more than we want to gain
- We remember negative events more than positive events
- We focus more on critical comments than positive feedback

The problem, of course, is that we now live in a world with very few real threats.

After all, the most common place we get "attacked" is on social media. The average distance to a McDonald's from home in the United States is three miles! And with modern transportation, it's relatively easy to leave one tribe and find another.

Yet we still have the cavedweller's brain, which is where goals come into play.

Goals Rewire Your Brain for Success

It turns out goals work like magic because they cognitively rewire our cave dwellers' brains. They modify and regulate our actions.

KEY POINT

Goals regulate action.

Researchers say that goals are effective for four key reasons:
1. effort/energy
2. direction
3. persistence
4. learning

First, goals inspire us to put forth more energy and effort. As mentioned previously, the bigger the goal, the more effort and energy we will exert to reach it. We'll push ourselves harder. For example, a jogger might exert herself just a little extra to achieve the time goal she set for a run. A writer might maximize their focus to write faster in order to hit a word count goal. If they have a weight training goal, someone doing resistance training will give it their all on the final rep. However, energy and effort are wasted if they are scattered about randomly. So...

Goals also serve to direct our efforts. This works in two ways. Goals direct our efforts towards goal-positive things and away from goal-negative things. Someone with a goal to lose weight is directed towards fruit and vegetables and away from fast food. Someone with a goal to save money is directed towards making more money, and away from spending money. Someone trying to build their side hustle will direct their Sunday time towards their business and away from watching football.

Third, goals increase our persistence (i.e., time spent on a task). A student who has a goal for better grades will study longer. A writer will work on her novel a little later into the night. The athlete will spend more time in the gym. Someone focused on weight loss will walk longer (more steps).

Fourth, goals stimulate our desire for knowledge and skills. We will seek to discover the best methods for achieving our goal. A financial goal may cause us to learn about 401k retirement accounts. A health goal may have us learning about vegan diets. A relationship goal may have us reading *Men Are From Mars, Women Are From Venus*, or worse, watching Dr. Phil.

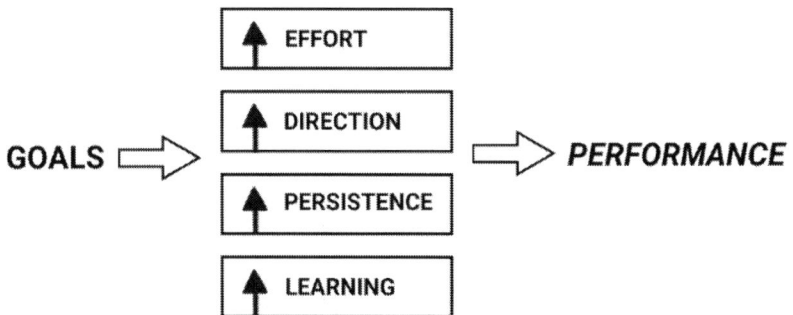

So now you know how goals rewire your lazy-keep-you-safe cave person brain.

Setting Goals versus Achieving Goals

I'll reveal the secrets to getting everything you ever wanted in the next chapter. But first, you need to realize that this comes in two parts:

- How you should set goals
- How you should pursue and ultimately achieve goals

We'll break it down further throughout the book.

Inspiration

"It is not the critic who counts, not the man who points out how the strong man stumbles or where the doer of deeds could have done them better. The credit belongs to the man who is actually in the arena, whose face is marred by dust and sweat and blood; who strives valiantly; who errs, who comes up short again and again because there is no effort without error and shortcoming, but who does actually strive to do the deeds; who knows great enthusiasms, the great devotions; who spends himself in a worthy cause; who at the best knows, in the end, the triumph of high achievement, and who at the worst, if he fails, at least fails while daring greatly, so that his place shall never be with those cold and timid souls who neither knows victory nor defeat."

–Theodore Roosevelt

POWER TWEETS FOR MOTIVATION

"Be bold, be fearless, be unstoppable! Conquer your fears and step into the unknown with confidence. Remember, every great achievement starts with a daring decision. Embrace your inner lion! #BeBold #FearlessLiving"

"Overcoming fear opens the door to endless possibilities. Face your fears, take that leap of faith, and watch your life transform. Life's greatest adventures await the bold! #FearlessMindset #EmbraceTheJourney"

"Fear is temporary, but regret lasts a lifetime. Embrace the challenges, take risks, and remember that fortune favors the bold. Don't let fear hold you back from creating a life you love! #BeBoldAndFearless #NoRegrets"

"Break free from the chains of fear and unleash your true potential. Boldness empowers you to dream bigger, push harder, and achieve greatness. Today is the day to stand tall and shine! #OvercomeFear #UnleashGreatness"

"Life is like a roller coaster: full of ups and downs, twists and turns. Embrace the thrill, conquer your fears, and enjoy the ride! Being bold means saying yes to life's adventures. #FearlessLiving #LifeIsARide"

SECRET #2

Without goals, you have a cave dweller brain
trying to keep you safe, not successful.

HOW MIGHT YOU APPLY THIS?

Goals help us to get past our fears of failure and judgment and reprogram our minds to increase our energy, direction, persistence, and learning.

- **NETWORK MARKETING PROFESSIONAL**: Goals can increase your time spent on social media posting and digital recruiting, developing your business builders while maintaining interest in your own ongoing growth.
- **SALES PROFESSIONAL**: Goals can be an effective way to get you to your 50 "touches" a day, to plow through the dreaded CRM data entry, and to learn what techniques are best for prospecting.
- **MANAGER / LEADER**: Goals can increase efforts to be both an engaging people-leader (e.g., take more of a coach approach and hold consistent one-on-one meetings) as well as achieve business results.
- **CREATIVE ENTREPRENEUR**: Goals can increase your social media post frequency, your messaging to followers, and your overall content creation.

- **INDIVIDUAL HEALTH**: Goals can increase your efforts to replace junk food with whole food, to get off the couch and onto the treadmill, to hit consecutive days of meditation.
- **ATHLETE**: Goals can increase your efforts to get better at throwing a change-up, grabbing rebounds, or just spending more time in the gym.
- **SPOUSE OR PARENT**: Goals can increase efforts to actually go on weekly date nights, spend quality time with your kids on Sunday mornings, or text friends on Fridays.
- **STUDENT**: Goals can increase your effort around studying, rehearsing for the school play, or applying to colleges.

Self-Coaching Or Book Club Questions

1. What specific fears or worries do you have about failure or embarrassment, and how are they holding you back?
2. Whose judgment are you most concerned about?
3. How can you reframe your perspective on failure or embarrassment and view them as opportunities for growth and learning?
4. Have you given up on prior goals because it felt too hard? Do you regret not sticking with it a bit longer?
5. Would your friends and family consider you lazy or a hard worker? Why?

Goal Big or Go Home!

What If Every Goal You've Ever Had Was Just Too D*mn Small?

"PEOPLE ARE NOT LAZY. THEY SIMPLY HAVE IMPOTENT GOALS—THAT IS, GOALS THAT DO NOT INSPIRE THEM." — TONY ROBBINS

"DREAM NO SMALL DREAMS, FOR THEY STIR NOT THE HEARTS OF MEN." — JOHANN WOLFGANG VON GOETHE

dream

A strongly desired goal or purpose.

In the previous chapters, you learned that science shows that goals work to maximize performance, and without them, we'll revert to fear-based thinking.

Based on Dr. Locke's work, you need to think about goal setting as a model with two parts:

- First, set goals that are challenging (i.e., big) and specific
- Second, optimize your chances of hitting your goals by optimizing feedback, ability, environment, and commitment.

This chapter addresses setting goals that are *big*.

"There is a linear relationship between the degree of goal difficulty and performance." **–Dr. Edwin Locke**

Storytime: Romantic New Year's Day Gone Wrong

New Year's Day, in a cute little bed and breakfast in Cape May, New Jersey. My then-wife and I rang in the new year and sat down for a "visioning" exercise. Over coffee and croissants, what should have been an inspiring bonding activity quickly turned into a foreboding fight.

We were financially broke at the time—no savings and budgeting our money just to make our monthly bills. I, of course, started jotting notes about how many millions we'd have in the bank in five years, and the kind of house we'd be living in, the cars we'd drive, the vacations we'd have. And I wanted to work backward from five years out to the present day to come up with annual plans, then quarterly.

The ideas and excitement were one way. She got quieter and quieter. Finally, she burst out, "Those aren't goals. Those are dreams. Those are fantasies! What's the point of talking about fantasies? We need to set a goal of saving $5,000 this year. We need to set a goal to paint the kitchen."

I was hurt, offended, and lacking any conflict resolution skills or empathy, I just shut down. The visioning exercise on New Year's Day was over; we checked out early and drove home in silence.

Five years later, I sold my startup for many millions of dollars. We were divorced a year later, and when she got half of everything and a little more, I was tempted to ask, "Do you still think my goals were just a fantasy?" I was nice enough not to have actually asked that out loud but wasn't nice enough not to have had the thought!

The Bigger The Goal, The Better We Perform

Researchers have shown in numerous studies that the harder the goal is, the better we perform, as long as we still think the goal is still achievable.

The graph below shows how performance continues to increase as the goal becomes more and more difficult—meaning bigger and bigger. That is, it increases right until the point where you no longer believe the goal is attainable, and then performance crashes because it seems hopeless.

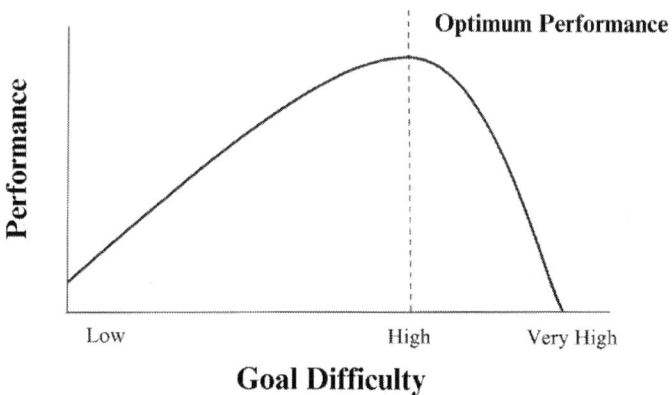

But How Big Is Too Big?

I can tell you that one of my single greatest mistakes in life has been that my goals are always too small.

Remember, I'm the guy who went from broke to millionaire by age 30, sold multi-million-dollar companies, and hit the *New York Times* bestseller list—and still, I'm telling you my goals were way too small.

How big your goals should be is tough because, just like beauty is in the eye of the beholder, the believability of goals is different from person to person. It doesn't matter if I think your goal is unrealistic or not. What matters is if you believe it's possible.

But again, most people set their goals way too small.

QUOTE

*"Most people overestimate what they can do in one year and underestimate what they can do in ten years." —**Bill Gates***

Storytime: My Totally Lame Goal to Become a Millionaire

My single biggest failure in business is that I repeatedly fail to set goals high enough. That's not a throwaway line.

I'm not just saying that in a general sense. Literally, while I spent five years in my twenties building a million-dollar business, two people I would later meet were building a $35 million and a $55 million business, respectively, all because they thought they could.

Let me start at the beginning...

I was born lower-middle class, and the adults I saw growing up were primarily electricians, painters, drywall hangers, and truck drivers. They were hard-working, honest, blue-collar workers.

I certainly don't remember ever knowing a doctor, a lawyer, an engineer, or any other six-figure professional until I was in my late teens. I think I had only ever met one person who was "rich," and that was the guy who owned the company my Dad worked in.

So my frame of reference was really small.

I was the first person in my family to ever go to college, and when I graduated, I was dead broke. I wanted to be financially independent, so I set my goal to have one million dollars by the age of 30.

And depending on your age and background, maybe you think setting a goal to become a millionaire sounds good.

But why one million dollars by age 30?

Why not $5 million?

Or why not by age 25?

Because that's all I could imagine was possible. It was my own constraint.

And indeed, a million dollars is a lot of money—I know that. And back then, at the age of 22, I had absolutely no idea how I was going to achieve it.

But that was the amount and time frame that it just seemed like I could figure it out. *I could see it as possible.*

I'm going to say that again. That goal was all that seemed possible to me. I didn't know how I could do it, but it seemed within the realm of possibility.

And you know what? I did it. I hit the goal. I became a millionaire at age 30.

But in the years to come, I would meet others who would show me that I had wasted valuable years pursuing a goal that was just too small.

How Two Mentors Generated $35 Million & $65 Million In 5 Years

To recap, when I was 21 years old and dead broke, having a business that made a million a year seemed impossible. How do I make a business? What do I sell? I had no idea where to start. Because a million dollars seemed impossible, it took me five years and a couple of failures before I figured out how to do it.

But then I sold my company to Raymond Karsan associates, and I saw how the CEO of that company, Rudy Karsan, built a company from zero to $35 million in revenues.

Wait a minute...in the same time period when I was growing a business from $0 to $1 million, you grew your business from $0 to $35,000,000?

And he seemed like a regular guy. I mean wicked smart, but just a man. And I could see how he did it. The year he bought my company, he bought twelve other small companies.

It was a strategy I learned was called a "roll up." If you had access to a good line of credit, knew how to stretch your vendors to maximize cash flow, and were wily enough to convince young entrepreneurs to merge their business with your own, you could "roll up" a $35 million dollar company in five years. I'm not saying it was easy, but once I saw how it was done, I knew it was a realistic goal.

I could have done all those things, too, during the same five years, but it just never occurred to me. It never occurred to me because I was achieving my goal year by year, doing what I knew how to do. I was happy crawling my way to a "measly" million dollars.

But meeting Rudy opened my eyes to how you build a $35 million business in five years. And I thought that was really remarkable.

And then I met Neil...

I started my next company with a small strategic investment from another business owner named Neil, who led a company called AXIS.

Neil, *in the same previous five years*, built his company from *$0 to $65 million*, and he did it without a single acquisition (i.e., he didn't buy up any companies along the way like Rudy did).

Neil's technique was to hire the number two leader from successful fast-growing companies and help them set up a new company where he owned 60%, and his new partner owned 40%.

He rightly guessed that many successful people don't actually like playing "second fiddle" and would jump at a chance to have the CEO title and a big chunk of a new company. He knew that a lot of very talented people who were great at what they do also had no interest in things like payroll, HR, leasing office space, etc. Neil also rightly guessed that these people would be able to bring a lot of clients and employees with them.

Here's the genius of Neil's approach: instead of paying top dollar to buy the whole company, he just paid a high salary, title, and equity to hire one key person!

He created eight different companies in five years with very little cash outlay.

$65 million! While my little lower-class brain was thinking a million dollars was a stretch goal, Neil was building a $65 million business from scratch.

Once again, I got to know Neil and saw him as a charismatic, bold visionary–who didn't mind fighting lawsuits related to non-compete agreements–but he didn't have a sky-high IQ or a fancy business degree. Once I saw that he could build a $65 million dollar company in five years, it was easy for me to "dream" of creating a hundred million company.

And you know what? There are plenty of examples from people I don't know who have accomplished so much more. If you're willing to look at the tech industry, Yahoo, Facebook, and Google all made over half a billion dollars after five years in business.

With my current company, LEADx, my goal is to create a $100 million company. I think I can do it in five years. Now that I know it's *possible*... I can believe it.

Oprah's Story

"I always knew I'd be a millionaire by age thirty-two. In fact, I am going to be the richest black woman in America...If you believe you can only go so far, it is an obstacle...Whatever your goal, you can get there if you're willing to work." –**Oprah Winfrey**
In 2022, Oprah's net worth was $2.6 billion (*Forbes*).

Big Goals for Health

Now maybe money and business aren't your things. Let me share a health example.

Health is my weakest area in life. I mean, I'm within normal weight and don't smoke or have any health problems, but my wish is to look like Zac Efron in Baywatch, and at age fifty-five, that hasn't miraculously happened yet.

My normal thing year after year is to say, "Whoa, my weight has crept to 180, and I'm pudgy. Time to lose five or ten pounds of fat and gain some muscle. No more Dad bod for me!"

So, I set the goal, hit the treadmill and weights more often, and started eating healthier, and I lost about a pound a week until I hit about 170 pounds. But then I started to think I don't look too bad, and I start traveling, and I think since I lost some weight, I can handle a bit more fast food and pizza, and voila, I'm back up to 180 pounds again.

My health goal is usually to lose around 5-10 pounds because that's my belief system. That's a pretty good weight to be at, and I struggle to do it, so that's the goal.

Well, just last week, I stumbled on an interview in *People* magazine with the actor Mark Wahlberg. In it, Wahlberg talks about how he lost 61 pounds for his role in the movie The Gambler. Sixty-one pounds! He went from a muscular 196 pounds down to 135 pounds.

Mark Wahlberg said, "I completely changed my training program and gave up wine, bread, and pasta. Now I'm eating small portions of protein throughout the day and jumping rope a lot."

Now, let me be clear...I'm not suggesting I or anybody else needs only to weigh 135 pounds. That sounds very unhealthy to me. And I'm not advocating for extreme diets that might jeopardize your health.

What I am saying is that while my little brain struggles with the goal of losing 5-10 pounds, others are dropping massive amounts of weight quickly. (I mean, have you seen the TV show Biggest Loser?) The point is that most of us set goals that are far too easy; the bar is set way too low.

"God-Sized" Goals And Spiritual Adrenaline

Luke Barnett is the Senior Pastor of Dream City Church, with its primary location in Phoenix, Arizona. I had the chance to talk to Luke on my podcast about his book, *The Dream-Centered Life*. He shared how he took over the church from his father and immediately fell into a depression. He didn't know how to emerge from his father's shadow or what to do. So he spent 40 days in reflection, and as he puts it, "God began to show me a picture of our future that produced passion inside of me."

And what a picture it was. He saw that ten years into the future, which would also be the church's 100-year anniversary, the church would:

Become the #1 art hub of Arizona

They would reach 50,000 people, even though they only served 5,000 people at the time.

They would train 100,000 leaders.

They would be debt free, even though they hadn't been debt free in a quarter of a century.

They would have multiple campuses.

Most people thought it was a pipe dream. But as of the writing of this book, with a little time left, Pastor Luke and Dream City Church have fulfilled or exceeded most of these goals.

In my hour-long chat with Luke, one phrase stood out to me. He explained that you need God-sized goals. You need to set goals so big you will not succeed without God's intervention. This, of course, is the exact opposite of the classic SMART goals formula most people are taught in which goals need to be "achievable."

Just as I don't really believe in "the secret," I'm not so sure there is a God that cares too much about my wealth, health, relationships, or the size of my business.

But! What an amazing lesson from Pastor Luke. If my continued failure is that I set my goals too low. My goals are too small. Then imagine what might have happened if I truly set goals so big I could not succeed without outside intervention.

At the very least, I would wake up every morning fired up with what Luke calls "spiritual adrenaline."

But What If The Goal Is *Too* Big?

Remember the graph earlier in this chapter. You want to set your goal to be as challenging as possible but still within the realm of believability. If it's too big or too complex, it will be less effective.

RESEARCH

A "complex goal" is 28% less effective than a "regular goal." (source: Wood, Mento & Locke, 1987).

So, what do you do if you have a dream, a goal, that you are struggling to believe in?

What if you have a big goal but really no knowledge of how even to begin pursuing it?

It's simple. You simply break your big goal down into smaller goals. These are called "subordinate goals."

In Their Own Words: Herbalife Network Marketers

What does it take to rise to the top levels of network marketing?

I asked this question to Fabiola Barinas and Alan Rodriguez, a married couple who are at the "Chairman's Club" level at Herbalife—the second highest level possible, which puts them into the elite .1% of all distributors.

Their story starts ten years ago when Barinas was a struggling actress and Rodriguez was working over sixty hours a week in multiple jobs. Frustrated by their lack of financial success—down to their final $2,500—and also frustrated by their inability to spend time together, they attended a Herbalife Nutrition Opportunity Meeting and decided to sign up.

Just two months after signing up, they went to the annual Herbalife Extravaganza event, where they heard multiple success stories from people with similar backgrounds to themselves. Barinas and Rodriguez decided to set a very ambitious goal to reach the top 1% level within five years.

Why five years? They picked that time frame because it was the average amount of time they heard that it took other people to achieve the goal. *Essentially, they perceived their goal as "achievable" due to the success stories shared by people similar to them.*

Rodriguez confessed initial skepticism regarding their ambitious target, attributing the visionary aspect of their mission to his wife, Barinas. What she could see a "possible" he initially saw as "impossible." Nonetheless, he concentrated on their interim objectives, which he calls "micro-goals." And with each milestone accomplished, his belief in the possibility of reaching their overarching five-year goal grew stronger. Indeed, they reached their goal in less than five years, and naturally set an even higher goal.

In Their Own Words: F1 Haas Team Principal Guenther Steiner

Guenther Steiner is an Italian motorsport engineer, an entrepreneur, and best known as the team principal of the Haas Formula One team. Steiner has gained notoriety since being featured prominently in the Netflix series Drive to Survive.

Unlike the other, more reserved team principals, Steiner's commentary is unfiltered and includes frequent F-bombs. One comment in particular— "We look like a bunch of wankers"—instantly became a catchphrase, went viral on social media, and is now emblazoned on t-shirts among his fans.

Steiner is credited with convincing Gene Haas to invest and launch the Haas Team in 2016. It's F1's newest team, and the only team located in the United States. I had a chance to talk to Steiner about having big, but realistic, goals. Here's what he said:

"If I would've told Mr. Haas when we started the F1 team, 'We will win our race in five years, or in three years,' That's not a realistic goal. And maybe he wouldn't have done the team then. But I told him, 'We are the latest one in. We need to work our way up. The second youngest team as it is now, is maybe 30 years old. So how can I come in there and tell you we're going to win races? I'd have to ask you for stupid amounts of money.' But I knew that he wouldn't want to do that. So my goal was, 'We will score points, we will be respectable, and we will work our way up.'"

Navy SEALs BUD/S Training – Get to Lunch

"Just get to lunch," I muttered to myself. It was the only way I could control my anxiety. In 1998, I'd made it through Basic Underwater Demolition/SEAL, or BUD/S, by focusing on just making it to the next meal. It didn't matter if I couldn't feel my arms as we hoisted logs over our heads or if the cold surf soaked me to the core. It wasn't going to last forever. There is a saying: "How do you eat an elephant?" The answer is simple: "One bite at a time." Only my bites were separated by meals: Make it to breakfast, train hard until lunch, and focus until dinner. Repeat." **–Mark Owens,** *No Easy Day*

Mark Owens had the big goal of surviving the grueling US Navy SEAL training program. If participants focus on the long path and pain ahead, they are very likely to "ring the bell," quit, and go home. So Owens broke his big goal down into subordinate goals. Make it to breakfast. Get to lunch. Survive until dinner.

People who train to run a marathon know this approach all too well. They don't set one goal to run a marathon and then just randomly go running as far as they can each day. A beginner with a six-month training plan might have the subordinate goal of running nine miles over four days in the first week. The second week would increase to ten miles, etc.

I had a goal throughout my twenties to write a book, but I never made much progress because the big goal seemed too daunting. Someone gave me advice, which I routinely give to other aspiring authors, to think of it as a series of blog posts or articles. I now have an annual goal to write a book, with ten subordinate goals to write ten chapters. Each chapter is a series of sections (articles, blog posts, whatever) which I create an action plan for.

QUOTE

"God's dream for your life is bigger than your own." –Joel Osteen

Takeaway

So let me repeat it: I continue to set my goals way too low throughout my career.

Remember, the bigger the goal, the more powerful the results, right up to the point where you don't think it's possible.

Jim Carrey's goal was a $10 million check. Oprah's goal was to be the richest Black woman in America. Most Olympic athletes have a goal from a young age to win a gold medal.

So, step one is to dream big. Whatever area of your life you want to improve—health, wealth, relationships, spirituality, career—stretch to make your goal a big one.

Remember, only you determine if your goal is possible and how big it should be. But remember, if it isn't big enough to get you excited every day—to get you to jump out of bed without a snooze hit—then you should set it bigger or pick a goal that is truly motivating.

POWER TWEETS FOR MOTIVATION

"Dream big, aim high, and reach for the stars! Big goals inspire greatness and ignite the fire within us. Don't settle for less; set your sights on the extraordinary! #DreamBig #BigGoalsBigSuccess"

"Big goals fuel our passion and drive us to achieve the unimaginable. Embrace your wildest dreams and remember that anything is possible with perseverance and determination. #ThinkBig #LimitlessPotential"

"Transform your world by dreaming big and setting monumental goals! Break free from the ordinary and challenge yourself to create a life beyond your wildest dreams. Be the architect of your own destiny! #DreamBigGoals #ChangeYourWorld"

"Shoot for the moon, and even if you miss, you'll land among the stars! Big goals propel us toward incredible achievements and inspire us to surpass our own expectations. Aim high and achieve greatness! #DreamBigAimHigh #GoForGreatness"

"Big goals are the seedlings of innovation, creativity, and progress. Dreaming big nurtures our ability to think outside the box and revolutionizes our world. Embrace your grandest aspirations and make history! #BigGoalsBigImpact #InnovateAndInspire"

SECRET #3

Goals should be as big as possible, as long as you believe they are actually achievable.

HOW MIGHT YOU APPLY THIS?

- **NETWORK MARKETING PROFESSIONAL**: What if instead of setting a goal to recruit five new members to your team in a month, your goal was to recruit 50 new team members?
- **SALES PROFESSIONAL**: What if instead of setting a goal to do 50 touches a day to prospects (e.g., email, LinkedIn, voicemail), your goal was 100?
- **MANAGER / LEADER**: What if instead of setting a goal to have your location achieve a good employee engagement score, your goal was to win a Best Place to Work award?
- **CREATIVE ENTREPRENEUR**: What if, instead of setting a goal to increase your follower count by 1,000 in the next month, your goal was to reach 1,000,000 followers within two years while establishing partnerships with major brands?

- **INDIVIDUAL HEALTH**: What if instead of setting a goal to go to the gym three times a week, your goal was to run a marathon within a year? Or an Iron Man in two years?
- **ATHLETE**: What if, instead of setting a goal to increase your three-point shooting percentage during practice, your goal was to become your team's top scorer?
- **SPOUSE OR PARENT**: What if, instead of setting a goal for a weekly date night, your goal was to feel more connected and in love with your partner than ever before—imagine if each year just got better and better.
- **STUDENT**: What if, instead of a goal to join an extracurricular club or activity, your goal was to become the club president or team captain?

Self-Coaching Or Book Club Questions

Find a quiet place at a time when you won't be interrupted and imagine all the things you'd like to achieve, have and do if there were no limits.

1. Fantasize about achieving different huge goals—which ones are the most exhilarating?
2. What are your financial goals? Do you want to pay off all your credit cards? Or have a six-figure salary? How about a six-figure annual passive income? Do you want to be a millionaire? Do you want toys of wealth: a plane, a yacht, a Porsche?
3. What are your relationship goals? Do you dream of getting married to your soul mate? Do you want to reconnect with your parents? Do you want an amazing relationship with your teenage kids? (Yes, it's possible, even teenagers!)
4. What are your health goals? Do you want to lose weight? Gain muscle? Improve mobility? Become a vegan?
5. Do you want to reconnect with God? Read the Bible, Koran, or Bhagavad Gita? Would you like to become a Sunday school teacher or experience the bliss of meditation?

6. How about your career? Do you want a raise, a promotion, or an advanced degree?

7. How do you want to give back? What do you want your legacy to be? Do you want to build schools for poor children in Africa? Do you want to create a scholarship fund for inner-city youth? Do you want to rescue 100 animals? What do you want to contribute to making a difference in your life?

The JFK Man On The Moon Formula

How the Power of Precision Unlocks Unprecedented Goal Success

"YOU CAN'T HIT A TARGET YOU DON'T HAVE." — ZIG ZIGLAR

"GENIUS IS IN THE DETAILS." — GUSTAVE FLAUBERT

---

spe·cif·ic

Free from ambiguity.

When John F. Kennedy announced that the United States would send a man to the moon, he didn't say, "I have a dream to send men into space."

He didn't even say, "We're going to put a man on the moon."

Instead, he announced a goal that was made powerful with a three-part structure.

This chapter will explore President Kennedy's Secret to Goal Specificity and revisit his famous declaration.

Setting Versus Pursuing Goals

When you think of using goals to transform your life, think about the process in two parts:

First, how to set goals properly (hint: they need to be challenging and specific)

Second, how to optimize your chances of hitting goals with a focus on ability, environment, feedback, and commitment.

This chapter addresses setting goals that are *specific.*

Dreams Are Vague; Goals Are Specific

Since most people don't understand the psychology of goal setting, they go about goals all wrong. They speak of vague desires like:

- I want to be rich
- I want to lose weight
- I want to marry my soul mate
- I want to retire early
- I want to own my own business
- I want to be famous

But wait a minute. You might be saying, why's that wrong? In the last chapter, you told me to dream big dreams and set big goals!

That's true. But Dr. Locke and other researchers found that goals without specificity allowed for a wide range of interpretations, which led to a wide range of "acceptable" effort and performance.

You can set a goal to "get healthy" or "do my best to lose weight," but without specificity, typically, there is little action and no results.

For example, a "lose 4 pounds in 4 weeks" goal is specific and measurable, leaving no discrepancy over your ultimate achievement.

A goal to "get four rebounds in the upcoming game" is better than "get more rebounds."

A goal to "have a net worth of $1 million in five years" is better than a goal "to be rich someday."

A 3-Part Formula For Goal Specificity

The more specific your goal, the better. For example, your goal statement could include the following:

- Measurement–what is the quantity of your goal? By how much?
- Time period–by when will you hit your goal?
- Conditions–under what conditions will you hit your goal?

QUOTE

"I believe that this nation should commit itself to achieving the goal, before this decade is out, of landing a man on the Moon and returning him safely to the Earth." –John F. Kennedy

A 3-Part Formula For Goal Specificity

In May of 1961, US President John Kennedy addressed Congress and declared the goal to put a man on the moon. Read his exact quote above. Notice he didn't just state a vague vision to "one day go to the moon" or "explore space." His national goal had three parts:

1. The measurable observable achievement: land a man on the moon
2. The time period: within nine years
3. A condition: and get him back safely!

Eight years later, with a mere five months left to achieve the goal, Neil Armstrong walked on the moon, and three days later, he and the other astronauts splashed down near Hawaii.

You can almost think of it as a template:

I will [achievement] by [date] with/without [conditions].

How could we restate the soft goal to "lose weight" as a specific goal? One example:

- *"I will lose 10 pounds by December 1, without counting calories."*

Or we could rewrite this health-related goal, "I will be more active this year," to:

- *"I will work out at the gym at least three days a week, with each workout being at least 20 minutes long."*

Here are some more examples of well-crafted goal statements:

- [Health] I will complete the New York City Marathon, on November 6, in under five hours.
- [Wealth] I will become debt free by January 1, 2025, while also saving 5% of my pay for retirement.
- [Relationship] We will have "date night" every week while taking turns choosing the activity.
- [Athlete] I will get four or more rebounds in tomorrow's game while still being the first one back on defense.
- [Education] I will maintain a 3.7 GPA during my junior year of high school while also playing varsity soccer.
- [Real Estate Career] I will send ten prospecting messages on Facebook daily, regardless of how many showings or closings I'm working on.
- [Sales Career] I will achieve over 50 touches each day, including email, LinkedIn, and phone channels.
- [Author] I will write 1,000 words daily before the kids wake up, except for Saturday and Sunday.
- [Network Career] I will add ten new people to my team by the end of the month, not including family members.

Daymond John Wants $102,345,086.32

Shark Tank star and founder of Fubu, Daymond John, not only has specific goals, he has a specific amount in mind. Similar to Jim Carrey, John once wrote down the goal of cashing a check for $102,345,086.32.

He says, "That's an actual number I wrote down with all my other goals, as a way to visualize what I wanted in a way that seemed real, not arbitrary. I'd rather hit a specific target than aim for a general area – that's why the bull's eye is worth more than all those other rings on the target."

Takeaway

I didn't do too badly when I set my first real goal, "I'll be a millionaire by age 30."

It was a specific, measurable achievement ($1,000,000) and a due date (by the time I turned 30).

But with thirty years of hindsight, it would have been strengthened with the final part, under what conditions? It could have been anything, for example:

- "...while maintaining a strong relationship with my wife."
- "...while working no more than 50 hours a week."
- "...and 80% of my assets are liquid assets."
- "...while staying true to my high ethical standards."

The research is clear: specific goals work better than vague or "do my best" goals. The more specific, the better

POWER TWEETS FOR MOTIVATION

"Details matter! When setting goals, specificity is key. Clearly defined objectives provide a roadmap to success, guiding each step of your journey. Be specific, stay focused, and achieve greatness! #SpecificGoals #PowerOfDetail"

"The power of detail lies in its ability to sharpen your focus. Specific goals create a clear vision, helping you channel your energy and resources effectively. Home in on the details and unlock your full potential! #SpecificityMatters #FocusedSuccess"

"Specific goals are the stepping stones to monumental achievements. By breaking down your dreams into detailed objectives, you can measure progress and celebrate each milestone. Small wins lead to big victories! #PowerOfSpecificGoals #MilestoneMoments"

"Transform your dreams into reality with the power of specificity! Detailed goals provide actionable steps, making even the most ambitious aspirations achievable. Embrace the details and make every moment count! #SpecificGoalsPower #DreamsToAction"

"Specific goals are the pieces that complete the puzzle of success. By focusing on the finer details, you create a vivid picture of your desired future. Let the power of detail and specificity guide you to greatness! #PuzzleOfSuccess #DetailsMatter"

SECRET #4

Goals need to be specific.

HOW MIGHT YOU APPLY THIS?

- **NETWORK MARKETING PROFESSIONAL**: Your three-part goal statement might look something like, "I will recruit 5 new members to my team [achievement], every month [time period], while only working during my lunch hour and on Sundays [conditions]."
- **SALES PROFESSIONAL**: Your three-part goal statement might look something like, "I will line up 5 new demos [achievement], each week [time period], separate from the demos handed to me by my SDRs [conditions]."
- **MANAGER / LEADER**: Your three-part goal statement might look something like, "My team will launch software version 4.6 [achievement], by the end of Q2 [time period], without anyone having to work more than 40 hours a week [conditions]."

- **CREATIVE ENTREPRENEUR**: Your three-part goal statement might look something like, "I will reach 100,000 YouTube subscribers [achievement], by January 1, 2025 [time period], without doing any collaborations [conditions]."
- **INDIVIDUAL HEALTH**: Your three-part goal statement might look something like, "I will lose 40 pounds [achievement], in 20 weeks [time period], while never going below 1550 calories a day [conditions]."
- **ATHLETE**: Your three-part goal statement might look something like, "I will increase my vertical jump by 3 inches [achievement], in 4 weeks [time period], by simply focusing on better technique [conditions]."
- **SPOUSE OR PARENT**: Your three-part goal statement might look something like, "We will have a two hour dinner date [achievement], each week [time period], without looking at our smartphones [conditions]."
- **STUDENT**: Your three-part goal statement might look something like, "I will achieve a 3.8 GPA [achievement], this semester [time period], while still participating in drama club [conditions]."

Self-Coaching Or Book Club Questions

1. Think about one or more goals you've had in the past that you failed to achieve. Were they specific goals or merely dreams?
2. What about goals you've set for yourself and achieved? Were they vague or specific?
3. What goals do you have right now that could be improved with the specificity of metrics, dates, and conditions?

The FFL Advantage

Achieve Your Goals Faster With Frequent Feedback Loops

"WE ALL NEED PEOPLE WHO WILL GIVE US FEEDBACK. THAT'S HOW WE IMPROVE." – BILL GATES

"IN ORDER FOR PEOPLE TO MAKE PROGRESS, THEY HAVE TO GET FEEDBACK AND INFORMATION ON HOW THEY'RE DOING." – DAN PINK

---

feed·back

The transmission of evaluative or corrective information about an action, event, or process to the original or controlling source.

You learned how to set challenging and specific goals in the previous section. Beginning with this chapter, you'll learn about the four "moderators" of goal performance. Basically, things impact whether you'll achieve your goal or not.

Dr. Locke and Dr. Latham identified four primary moderators of the impact of goal setting on performance:

- Feedback

- Commitment
- Ability
- Situation (i.e., environment).

In this chapter, we'll focus on maximizing feedback.

QUOTE

"Feedback is critical to goal effects because it enables people to track progress so that effort and strategy can be adjusted to attain the goal." – Dr. Edwin Locke

---

Feedback Drives Effort And Strategy

Let's start with an obvious simple example.

Let's say it's January first, and your New Year's resolution is to lose twelve pounds by the end of the year. So, month after month, you do things you think will lead you to that weight loss goal. And at the end of the year, you hop on a scale and–drumroll please–you only lost two pounds. Bummer!

But what if you had hopped on the scale at the end of June? Perhaps you would have seen you only lost one pound, and to reach your goal, you'd better try harder or try new strategies for the next six months. Even then, it would be a lot harder–after all, instead of needing to lose a pound a month, you'd have to lose almost two pounds a month.

A better approach would be to get on the scale to check your weight every month or even every week. With this frequent feedback, you would get answers to the questions:

- Am I making progress toward my goal?
- Am I behind or ahead of schedule to achieve my goal?
- Is what I'm doing to lose weight working or not?

And you would then have time to adjust your effort and strategy accordingly. If you were behind schedule after a few months pursuing your weight loss goal you might think:

- Walking 5,000 steps a day isn't enough; I'll increase it to 10,000 steps a day (effort)
- Cutting out desserts alone isn't working, so I'll cut out alcohol too and see if that increases results (strategy)
- Consuming 2,000 calories a day doesn't seem to be having any impact; I'll go down to 1,800 calories a day (effort)
- Just trying to cut down on snacking hasn't worked, I'll join Weight Watchers (strategy)

RESEARCH

While the above example may seem obvious, that hasn't stopped people from proving it. In fact, researchers conducted a study of 162 overweight individuals. All participants were taught evidence-based strategies for weight loss, and all were encouraged to try to reduce calories by about 100 calories per day. Then the participants were split into two groups. People in one group were given scales and told to weigh themselves daily. The other was not given these instructions.

After one year, the group that weighed themselves daily had lost an average of six pounds, while the other group only lost an average of one pound each. A daily feedback loop to a 600% improvement in result!

Feedback Can Be Quantitative Or Qualitative

The easiest and most accurate form of feedback is quantitative feedback. You simply measure your progress in the same way you intend to measure whether you ultimately achieved your goal.

For health goals, your quantitative measures might be your weight measured on a scale, cholesterol level from a blood test, body mass index measured with calipers, resting heart rate measured with an Apple watch, etc.

But qualitative feedback can be as important or even more important. Qualitative health-related goals might be selfie pictures you take in the mirror to see how your appearance is changing over time, how your clothes fit you, or how much more energy you have.

Qualitative feedback can also take the form of feedback from other people. You may be a salesperson with a goal of increasing your closing ratio. You might ask your sales manager to listen to your sales calls and give you feedback on your use of a "trial close" technique. In the spirit of coaching as feedback, here are more examples:

- A student with a GPA goal might want to ask their teachers for feedback on whether they are on track or not to get their desired grade
- Someone with a health goal might want to ask a dietician for feedback on their meal diary
- A network marketing professional with a goal of reaching World Club might ask someone already at that level to critique their business plan

In Their Own Words: Endurance Racer Phil Hanson

Phil Hanson is a 24-year-old British race car driver who has made significant strides in the world of endurance racing. One of Hanson's remarkable achievements was his outstanding performance in 2020, where he and his team became the first ever to win the European Le Mans Series, World Endurance Championship, and the prestigious 24 Hours of Le Mans, all in the same year. I talked to Hanson about his approach to goal setting and using feedback loops.

> *"During the race, you can assess not only your performance compared to your teammates' previous stints but also against all the other drivers on track fighting against you. This is reflected in what's called a stint average, which is an outcome. Some drivers can become fixated on stint averages, as it's easy to manipulate them to look exceptionally good or bad at the expense of achieving the ultimate goal [of winning the race]. Nevertheless, you can get a general understanding of your strength. All this data is provided to us live as we're racing, and then we can review it afterward in the reports. There's no hiding from the facts and data. If you haven't performed, it's there for the world to see; if you have, it's also evident."*

Storytime: The 'Idiots' Digging The Panama Canal

David McCullough tells a story in his book *Path Between the Seas* about the Panama Canal project. In 1907, George Washington Goethals became the project leader after the United States took over from the French in 1904. One of the things Goethals did to improve morale and camaraderie among workers was to launch a weekly newspaper called the Canal Record. The purpose of the newspaper was to provide accurate information based on official records about the progress of the canal construction.

Shortly after the Canal Record was published, there was a significant increase in productivity. The reason for this was that the newspaper listed the amount of tons excavated by each steam shovel team, and the teams began competing with each other to achieve the highest amount of excavation.

What is fascinating about this story is that the workers were not asked to work any differently, and their managers did not ask them to do more. The workers increased their productivity on their own due to their competitive instincts.

One worker described what happened:

"It wasn't so hard before they began printing the Canal Record. We were going along, doing what we thought was a fair day's work...but then away we went like a pack of idiots trying to get records for ourselves."

Takeaway

The key takeaway from this chapter is that having frequent feedback will significantly improve your chances of achieving your goals. So the critical question to answer after you set a challenging and specific goal is: how will I get feedback?

More specifically, what tool(s) will I use to get feedback? Examples of health goal tools include a scale, calorie tracking apps like MyFitnessPal, exercise apps like Strong, a blood pressure cuff, or a blood test. If you have a financial goal, your "tools" for measurement might be your monthly bank statement, or Quicken, or apps like Mint or NerdWallet.

Don't forget that pencil and paper or an Excel spreadsheet are great tools too! You can manually count the number of date nights you fit in each quarter with your spouse, how many words you've learned in a new language, or how many rebounds you got per game.

And how will you get qualitative feedback? Your own thoughts and feelings should always count. But is there a coach, family member, or trusted friend who can give you objective feedback related to your goal?

POWER TWEETS FOR MOTIVATION

Feedback is the catalyst for growth! Embrace it with open arms, for it sharpens your skills and illuminates the path to success. Keep learning, keep improving! #FeedbackMatters #GrowthMindset

Constructive feedback is a gift that guides you towards excellence. Cherish every opportunity to learn and refine your craft.

Remember, a diamond only shines after being polished! #EmbraceFeedback #ShineBright

Feedback builds bridges between your current self and your future potential. Treat it as a valuable asset in your journey of self-improvement. Success awaits those who learn and adapt! #FeedbackIsFuel #LevelUp

Feedback is the mechanism that turns good into great. Embrace every critique as a chance to evolve and reach new heights. Soar higher with the power of feedback! #RiseAbove #ContinuousImprovement

Each piece of feedback is a puzzle piece that completes your journey towards success. Assemble the knowledge and wisdom that others share, and watch your dreams take shape. #FeedbackForGrowth #UnlockYourPotential

SECRET #5

Quantitative and qualitative Frequent Feedback Loops are critical to goal success.

HOW MIGHT YOU APPLY THIS?

- **NETWORK MARKETING PROFESSIONAL**: In network marketing, you could create routines to get feedback from downline team members (what attracted them to you and your team), your team leader, and others who have had success.

- **SALES PROFESSIONAL**: To increase the number of demos scheduled from your outbound sales efforts, use data to refine your outbound tactics including subject lines and body copy, ask your manager to critique your phone calls, and consider getting a coach or mentor. Consider using call recording and analysis software like Gong or Avoma which can give you feedback on your speaking pace, use of verbal fillers, and more.

- **MANAGER / LEADER**: To improve your team's culture, use employee engagement data for feedback, and consider feedback from an executive coach.
- **CREATIVE ENTREPRENEUR**: As a creative, use quantitative feedback like post engagements to learn what your audience wants; get qualitative feedback from other creatives who have built larger channels than your own.
- **INDIVIDUAL HEALTH**: For health, there are countless ways to gather quantitative feedback. You could track your steps, your weight, your body fat percentage, your cholesterol, your vertical leap, time to run a mile, number of max pushups, etc. For qualitative feedback consider things like your energy level.
- **ATHLETE**: For athletes there are countless statistics based on your sport, your body composition, and your personal bests in the gym. For qualitative feedback consider asking your coach, "What's the #1 thing I should be working on right now?"
- **SPOUSE OR PARENT**: Try asking your partner this question, "So on a scale from one to ten, with ten being perfect. How was I as a husband/wife this week." And when they don't answer 10, ask this follow-up question, "What would I have done differently to make you answer a ten?"
- **STUDENT**: The single best thing you can do to boost your grades is to approach your teachers after class, or during their office hours, and ask a question similar to, "My goal is to get an A in this class. Can you give me advice on what I need to do to achieve that?" They might give you specific advice, but even if they don't, you'll stand out from the other students in the class and they'll believe you care. It could make a difference when they're using any level of subjectivity when grading your work.

Self-Coaching Or Book Club Questions

1. How open are you to receiving feedback? Are you able to receive it with an open mind?

2. When has someone given you feedback at work that immediately improved your performance?

3. When has someone given you feedback in your personal life that led to a positive outcome?

4. Think about goals you failed to achieve in the past. Were you tracking your progress? How? How often?

5. What are your current goals, and how are you measuring progress toward them? Are you tracking the right metrics, or are there other indicators you should focus on?

Unbreakable Resolve

16 Secrets to Sustaining Unwavering Commitment

"THE ONLY LIMIT TO YOUR IMPACT IS YOUR IMAGINATION AND COMMITMENT." —STEPHEN COVEY

"COMMITMENT IS THE FOUNDATION OF GREAT ACCOMPLISHMENTS." —HEIDI REEDER

com·mit·ment

The state or an instance of being obligated or emotionally impelled; an agreement or pledge to do something in the future.

Remember, Dr. Locke and Dr. Latham identified four moderators that strengthen or weaken the power of goals: feedback, commitment, ability, and situation. In this chapter, we'll focus on maximizing commitment.

QUOTE

"It is virtually axiomatic that a goal that a person is not really trying for is not really a goal and

therefore cannot have much effect on subsequent action." –Dr. Edwin Locke

Storytime: My Graveyard Of Abandoned Goals

They say we often end up teaching or even preaching about the things we most need to be reminded of ourselves, which is probably why I decided to write a book about goal setting. I've failed to reach my goals often in the past. For example:

- I had a goal to finish writing this book by the end of 2022. I even got an Airbnb down in Miami for a multi-week writing retreat. But I didn't work much on the book. (Visiting Art Basel and walking along the beach sure was fun, though!)
- I had the goal to "get down" to 168 pounds in 2022. Instead, the scale reached a new high as I met the clinical definition of being "overweight" and officially had a skinny-fat Dad-bod. (Did you know you can buy Dad-bod t-shirts–tight on top and loose in the belly.)
- I had the goal to meditate for twenty minutes a day. I skipped most days, and when I did meditate, it was often for just five to 10 minutes.

We often start with the best of intentions, and then day by day, week by week, our commitment wanes. And when we lose commitment, we lose the consistency of action.

The truth is that any worthy goal is going to take an incredible amount of commitment. It's easier to stay the same. It's easier not to change.

Can you relate? Perhaps you don't want to be a writer, but maybe you've failed to reach your side-hustle goals. Or your savings goals? Maybe you aren't trying to hit a weight-loss goal, but perhaps you tried to hit a workout goal but stopped going to the gym. Maybe you declared you're a vegan, and then that pepperoni pizza showed up? Maybe your goal is to start dating again, but it's so much easier to sit on the couch in your pajamas watching Project Runway.

We all have more abandoned goals than accomplished goals. And in almost every case, it's because we've lost commitment.

Let's *commit* to understanding why we lose commitment and how we can strengthen our commitment muscle in the future.

3+1 Psychological Killers Of Commitment

Researchers have identified literally dozens of variables that influence our commitments to our goals. And Dr. Locke identified the biggest factors to be social influence, goal conflict, and incentives, in that order. Let's review them one at a time.

1. **Social Influence: The Power of Peer Pressure**

   Peer pressure can be a double-edged sword. On one hand, it can be a powerful motivator, pushing us to strive for excellence and achieve our goals. After all, we want to keep up with the Jones! Or a modern-day equivalent might be, let's keep up with the Kardashians or other influencers we're addicted to following on social media. On the other hand, social influence can be a destructive force, causing us to doubt ourselves and second-guess our choices.

   If you have a goal to exercise regularly, but your friends don't share your enthusiasm for fitness, they may discourage you from pursuing your goal or ridicule you for it. You'll be in trouble if you try to lose weight and your friends like to have fun by drinking and gobbling nachos at the local Applebee's. In such a scenario, the influence of others can undermine your commitment and make it challenging to stay focused on what you want to achieve.

2. **Goal Conflict: When Your Goals Are at Odds**

   Goal conflict occurs when we have different goals that are in opposition to each other. For example, if you have a goal to exercise regularly, but you also have a goal to spend more time with your family, these goals may conflict with each other. Your partner just wants to sit on the couch and watch Netflix, and you want to walk outside for ninety minutes to get your 10,000 steps in. This can make it challenging to stay committed to both goals, as you may feel like you have to choose between one or the other. In such a situation, conflicting goals can lead to indecision and a lack of commitment, making it difficult to achieve either goal.

3. **Incentives: The Power of Pain and Pleasure**
    Incentives play a critical role in our commitment to our goals. Incentives can be either positive or negative, and they influence our behavior by providing us with a sense of pain or pleasure.

    For example, if you are a salesperson who is supposed to sell a million dollars for your quota, exceeding that goal will likely bring you a large bonus, while missing that goal could get you fired. Those are powerful incentives and are likely to keep you focused!

    But what about other areas of your life? Thousands declare resolutions to lose weight or hit the gym each New Year's Eve or Day. But most stop trying after a month. Perhaps it's because they were focused on the pain of doing the work, and they really weren't experiencing any pleasure—at least in the short term—from all the effort. This example brings up the point of different time horizons. Often when we choose a goal that will take new or extra effort, the short-term only brings discomfort. It's the long-term that brings pleasure.

In addition to Dr. Locke's big three reasons above, I think it's worth mentioning one other killer of commitment: perfectionism. You may be guilty of "all or nothing" thinking. Do you ever think, "Well, I might as well get dessert since I already ate those French fries?" And then, "I blew my diet last night, so I'll just restart it next week." Some perfectionists never get started at all, as they feel they need to have a perfect plan. Perfectionism is a perfect way to weaken your commitment muscle.

Storytime: My Big Wins

Earlier in this chapter, I shared three goals that I failed to achieve: finishing this book, losing weight, and meditating. But since then, I did complete two of the three goals.

- On January 1, I recommitted to my health and lost over 10% of my body weight in the last 100 days.
- I finally completed this manuscript on my birthday, May 2, and moved on to publishing tasks required to release it to the world.

So, what changed? Why did I suddenly accomplish two of the goals I previously failed? It's as if Dr. Locke himself had coached me to increase my commitment.

First, I **increased social commitment** by hiring not one but two fitness coaches. Additionally, my partner Christine hired a coach and pursued similar health goals. It's far easier to suffer when you're suffering together! I didn't make a big deal about it, but I did talk about my new healthy habits to my kids and colleagues. I also told more people that I was very close to finishing this book, and I started reconnecting socially with my author friends.

Second, I **reduced goal conflict** by temporarily eliminating any goals related to my company, LEADx. This was hard. Obviously, I still had to work hard at "my day job." But I detached myself from striving for any revenue growth goals and gave myself permission to work a lot less than normal. (Which means like 60 hours a week instead of 80.)

Regarding the third factor related to **pain and pleasure incentives,** I must admit that I struggle with celebrating my achievements or rewarding myself positively. But if I'm honest, I am getting positive emotions from having to buy new pants with two inches smaller waist. I feel good getting closer to helping more people with this book and getting closer to having more passive income hit my bank account month after month.

So why have I not achieved my daily meditation goal? Simply put my commitment to it has been lacking. To address this issue in the future, I might need to hire a meditation coach or join an online "sangha" that meets virtually every day to meditate. Additionally, I will need to change how I think about the time spent meditating. Instead of viewing it as time taken away from working on my other goals, I will need to see it as a means to help me achieve my other goals by improving my focus. It will also be essential to continue meditating long enough to experience the positive outcomes of improved focus and equanimity.

5 Social Strategies to Skyrocket Goal Commitment

There is a saying that you are the average of the five people closest to you. This is another way of saying that social influence is the number one driver of commitment to goals. So how can you use this to our advantage? Consider these strategies:

1. **Public Declarations:** Share your goals with friends, family, or even on social media. By publicly committing to your objectives, you create a layer of accountability that fuels your motivation and helps you stay on track.

2. **Accountability Buddies:** Find someone who shares similar goals or has a vested interest in your success. This partnership can provide mutual support and encouragement, turning the pursuit of individual goals into a collective endeavor.

3. **Social Support Networks:** Engage in online communities or local groups centered around your goals or interests. These networks offer invaluable resources, advice, and camaraderie, fostering an environment conducive to success.

4. **Role Models, Coaches, & Mentors:** Surround yourself with people who inspire you and have achieved the goals you're striving for. Their insights and experiences can provide guidance, while their accomplishments serve as powerful motivator.

5. **Celebrate Success & Embrace Feedback**: Share your progress and achievements with your social circle and invite constructive

feedback to refine your approach. This exchange bolsters your commitment and contributes to a culture of growth and continuous improvement.

---

6 Strategies to Crush Goal Conflict

Goal conflict is so pervasive there are numerous idioms that warn of this danger, including:

- You can't kill two birds with one stone.
- You can't chase two rabbits at the same time.
- You can't have your cake and eat it too.

Consider these strategies to reduce the chance of goal conflict.

1. **Prioritize Your Goals**: Determine which goals are most important to you and rank them in order of priority. This clarity will enable you to allocate your resources effectively and reduce the likelihood of conflicting goals.

2. **Align Your Goals**: Ensure that your goals are congruent with your values and overall life vision. Aligning your objectives with what truly matters to you fosters a sense of purpose and reduces the risk of internal conflicts that may hinder your commitment.

3. **Break Down Goals into Manageable Steps**: Divide your larger goals into smaller, actionable steps. This approach makes your objectives more attainable and minimizes the chances of becoming overwhelmed by conflicting demands.

4. **Set Realistic Timelines:** Establishing reasonable timeframes for your goals allows you to balance multiple objectives without overtaxing your resources. This reduces the pressure of conflicting deadlines and helps you maintain focus on each goal individually.

5. **Regularly Review & Adjust Your Goals:** Periodically evaluate your goals and progress, and make adjustments as necessary. This ongoing reflection enables you to identify potential conflicts early and adapt your approach to maintain your commitment and momentum.

6. **Communicate with Stakeholders:** When your goals involve others, clear communication is crucial to ensure that everyone is aligned and working towards the same objectives. This proactive approach can preempt potential conflicts and foster a collaborative atmosphere.

---

5 Strategies to Leverage Incentives and Disincentives

What is the reward for achieving your goal? Is it financial or emotional? Will it increase your pride and confidence? Will it help you to sleep better at night? What is the pain of not achieving your goal? Consider these strategies:

1. **Set Milestones:** Break down your goals into smaller, achievable milestones. Celebrate each success with a reward that you find personally meaningful, such as a treat, a day off, or a special purchase. These incentives reinforce your progress and fuel your motivation to continue.

2. **Establish Consequences:** Create consequences for not meeting your goals or milestones, such as skipping a favorite activity or making a donation to a cause you don't support. These disincentives are powerful reminders of the importance of staying committed to your objectives.

3. **Visualize Success:** Envision the outcomes of achieving your goals, and imagine the positive emotions and benefits that will accompany your success. This visualization can be a potent incentive, driving your commitment and motivation.

4. **Customize Your Incentives:** Tailor your personal preferences to ensure they resonate with your unique interests and passions. Creating meaningful rewards will heighten your motivation and strengthen your commitment to your goals.

5. **Evaluate and Adjust:** Regularly assess the effectiveness of your incentives and disincentives, making adjustments as needed to maintain their motivational impact. This ongoing reflection ensures

that your rewards and consequences remain relevant and compelling.

POWER TWEETS FOR MOTIVATION

The power of commitment is transformative. It turns dreams into reality, obstacles into steppingstones, and doubt into determination. Stay committed to your goals, and witness the magic unfold! ☐ #CommitToGreatness

Commitment is the anchor that keeps you grounded amidst the storms of life. Embrace it, and watch your dreams set sail! ☐ #UnleashYourPotential #CommitToWin

No goal is out of reach when fueled by unwavering commitment. Be steadfast in your pursuit; success will follow you like a shadow. ☐ #PowerOfCommitment #SuccessMindset

Commitment is the seed of progress. Plant it in the fertile soil of hard work and dedication and watch your dreams blossom into reality. ☐ #CommitAndConquer #GrowthMindset

Doubt may whisper, but commitment roars. Silence your fears by staying true to your path and let the power of commitment propel you to success. #RoarToVictory #FearlessCommitment

SECRET #6

Increase goal commitment by maximizing social support and incentives while minimizing goal conflict.

HOW MIGHT YOU APPLY THIS?

- **SALES OR NETWORK MARKETING PROFESSIONAL**: Maximize social support by surrounding yourself with high-achievers and mentors who inspire you to reach new heights. Ensure your family is aligned with your big goals and understand the sacrifices you'll make to achieve them. Tackle goal conflicts head-on by prioritizing tasks that align with your objectives, such as striking a balance between prospecting and nurturing clients. Finally, stay focused on the incentives that you find most motivating (e.g., free product, commission checks, top of the leader board, or making President's Club or Platinum Level).

- **MANAGER / LEADER**: It can be hard to remember to spend time on the "people stuff" amidst the daily pressure to "get stuff done." Who can be a positive social influence? Reflect on the best boss you ever had. Consider hiring an executive coach. When it comes to goal conflict, consider a balance between hitting your key performance indicators (KPIs) and having high employee engagement scores. Keep in mind the rewards for great leadership—some might include maxing out your bonus or getting a promotion, but what about the emotional rewards that come with being a great boss?

- **CREATIVE ENTREPRENEUR**: Connect with like-minded creatives and attend masterminds to maintain a positive social influence. Address goal conflicts by balancing daily content creation with follower engagement. Choose motivating incentives or small rewards as you hit specific follower counts, new levels of post engagement, or ad revenue.

- **INDIVIDUAL HEALTH**: In a world that celebrates drinking, food, and binging Netflix achieving health and wellness goals can be especially challenging. Can a neighbor meet you outside at 6:00 am to walk 10,000 steps with you? Should you hire a fitness coach to train you at home? Are your health goals in conflict with other work or social life goals? How much time each week should you allocate to each area? How will you reward yourself when you lose ten pounds? New wardrobe when you lose twenty?

- **ATHLETE:** Train alongside driven teammates and seek guidance from experienced mentors for positive social influence; always ask your coach what the number one thing you should be working on is to get better. Tackle goal conflicts by scheduling time for everything that matters: gym workouts, team practice, skill development, and recovery. Student-athletes need to embrace both studying and sports. Set rewards and celebrate wins along the journey, like achieving personal bests in the gym, making the team, or just improving your three-point percentage.

- **SPOUSE OR PARENT**: To strengthen your commitment to an emotionally strong marriage or other relationship, consider spending more time with couples who seem to be thriving. Gain additional support from marriage retreats or couples groups at your place of worship. Don't forget to make time for date nights or other rituals for connection in the everyday busyness of work, parenting, fitness, and chores. Make sure you balance your "me time" goals with your relationship goals. Don't forget to celebrate together, whether it's your anniversary, work promotions, or remodeling the kitchen.

- **STUDENT**: High school and college students have incredible potential distractions as they strive to hit their desired GPA or make Honors Society. Maintain strong social support by hanging out with friends with similar goals; consider forming study groups of like-minded friends. Be intentional about goals in different areas of your school life. If you're a student-athlete and president of the drama club, how much time will you allocate to each every week? How will you reward yourself for achieving milestones along the way?

Self-Coaching Or Book Club Questions

1. Think of a goal that you failed to achieve in the past. How committed were you to achieving it?

2. Think of a goal that you failed to achieve in the past. How much support did you have from family, friends, or work colleagues?

3. Think of a goal that you failed to achieve in the past. Were you more committed to achieving a different goal at the same time?

4. How will you feel when you accomplish your goal?

5. Will you be embarrassed or ashamed if you don't reach your goal?

6. Who can you ask to be your accountability partner?

7. Who doesn't support your goals? How can you win over their understanding and support?

8. Are any of your most important goals in direct conflict with each other?

9. What will you lose if you don't hit your goal?

10. How can you reward yourself when you achieve your goal? What mini rewards can you set up for milestones achieved along the way?

The Interplay Between Ability and Aspiration

Level Up Your Learning To Level Up Your Goals

"IT IS POSSIBLE TO FLY WITHOUT MOTORS. BUT NOT WITHOUT KNOWLEDGE AND SKILLS." —WILBUR WRIGHT

"BY FAR, THE BEST INVESTMENT YOU CAN MAKE IS IN YOURSELF. IF YOU INVEST IN YOURSELF, NOBODY CAN TAKE IT AWAY FROM YOU." —WARREN BUFFET

abil·i·ty

Competence in doing something.

Remember, Dr. Locke and Dr. Latham identified four primary moderators of the impact of goal setting on performance:
* Feedback
* Commitment
* Ability
* Situation (i.e., environment).

In this chapter, we'll focus on maximizing ability.

QUOTE

"People cannot attain goals if they do not know how to do so." –Dr. Edwin Locke

---

Taking Knowledge For Granted

Just before I started writing this chapter, I was procrastinating by scrolling through Twitter on my phone. A financial guru sent out a tweet that said something like:

Compound interest is the 8th wonder of the world. If you invest $100 a month into a mutual fund at 10% annual return you'll have half a million dollars in 40 years!

Or something like that.

Which is true and to me, obvious.

But then I read all the comments beneath the tweet. People sincerely asked questions like:

- "But how do I do that?"
- "What is a mutual fund?"
- "Where can I send my $100 - do you have an address?"

It would be easy to laugh at these questions, but they stopped me dead in my tracks. I clearly had the privilege of having a father who taught me about compound interest from a young age. I learned in my twenties how to set up accounts at Fidelity or Schwab and how to buy mutual funds.

Those comments on Twitter showed me that there are a lot of people who have zero knowledge of the basics that go into saving for retirement. What kind of financial future can they have when they don't have this basic knowledge?

Stating The Obvious

The idea that you must know how to do something in order to achieve it seems insultingly obvious. In fact, I almost didn't even include this goal moderator in this book.

Of course, if you set a goal to become the world's best chess player, and you don't know how to play chess, you are doomed to failure.

Similarly, if you set yourself a goal to save a million dollars for retirement and you have no knowledge at all of how interest works, or compound interest, or stocks, bonds, or mutual funds, the odds are stacked against you.

But, the power of this goal moderator is in the idea of increasing your *ability*–increasing your knowledge and skills related to your goals.

It's Time To Level Up .

While it's easy to understand that having no ability will lead to failure, few people realize how powerful gaining new knowledge can be. We need to think about the ability modifier as a form of "leveling up."

QUOTE

"Always keep learning. You stop doing useful things if you don't learn." **–Satya Nadella**

To use a video game metaphor, think about learning new things and gaining new skills as a way to "level up" and achieve higher levels in the game (your goals).

Earlier in this book, I shared how my first financial goal was to earn a million dollars by age 30. It's because I had no idea how to do it that I set such a small goal and barely reached it.

After that, I gained the knowledge that you can acquire companies with very little or no cash outlay at all. Then I learned that you could poach key talent from competitors as perhaps an even better way to build massive businesses quickly. If I had known about those things at age 25, I probably would have set a much bigger goal.

Here's an example of applying the video game metaphor to fitness goals. (And don't message me you fitness fanatics–I'm just using this as an example!) After someone sets a Big Specific Goal, how can someone dramatically increase their odds of losing weight and gaining strength by "leveling up" their knowledge?

- Level 1: Basic understanding that they should eat less and move more
- Level 2: Understanding how to calculate maintenance calories, appropriate daily caloric deficits, and how you need to burn 3,500 calories to lose a pound of fat
- Level 3: Understanding macros and different nutrition plans from 40/40/20 (my favorite) to Keto
- Level 4: Understanding how much protein to target to build or maintain muscle
- Level 5: Knowing how to do a variety of resistance exercises properly and how often to hit each muscle group
- Level 6: Knowing what High-Intensity Interval Training (HIIT) and Low-Intensity Steady State (LISS) are and the pros and cons of each

You can see clearly how ability in the area of fitness would greatly improve their odds of success.

Here's an example of leveling up abilities for a student trying to achieve good grades:

- Level 1: Some understanding that you must study to get good grades
- Level 2: Understanding of scheduling, time blocking, and other time management skills
- Level 3: Understanding how to minimize distractions and maximize focus

- Level 4: Understanding the pros and cons of study groups and study buddies
- Level 5: Understanding memory techniques
- Level 6: Knowing how to speed read

RESEARCH

Dr. Locke also found that not only does increasing your ability increase the chance you'll achieve your goal, but it can also cause you to choose a more ambitious goal!

Read that research call-out above again. It's super important. In fact, ability is such a strong factor that Dr. Locke and Dr. Latham say you are often better off setting a performance goal *after* you first set a learning goal.

Especially if you are pursuing something that is new to you, you literally don't know what you don't know. First create a learning goal to understand what is involved then set a new goal that will more than likely be bigger than the one you would have set originally.

My Most Recommended Level-Ups

My "3 to Thrive" are health, wealth, and relationships. Here are my favorite "level ups" for each.

When it comes to health, things that I learned that helped me the most include:

- What macros are and how to "hit them" every day
- The benefits (and challenges) of a plant-based diet
- The difference between high-intensity interval cardio (HIIT) and low-intensity steady-state (LISS)
- Proper technique and volume for resistance training
- The importance of sleep quality over quantity

- The importance of things in your blood like Vitamin D, B12, and testosterone
- Why and how to meditate

When it comes to building and keeping wealth, things that I learned that helped me the most include:

- The evils of debt
- "Pay yourself first" method of saving
- The power of compound interest
- Low-fee index funds
- The benefits of a fee-only financial advisor

QUOTE

*"Invest three percent of your income in yourself (self-development) in order to guarantee your future." –**Brian Tracy***

When it comes to business, things that I learned that helped me the most include:

- How to hire star performers
- All the different sales models (feature-benefit, Strategic Selling, SPIN Selling, Value-based Selling, Challenger Selling, etc.)
- How to write compelling headlines and hooks for marketing
- How to build a community
- How to give a great speech
- How to raise money from outside investors
- How to manage people so they feel engaged and motivated at work
- The power of SaaS companies to maximize valuation
- SaaS metrics to manage the business

When it comes to relationships, things that I learned that helped me the most include:

- Personality types (especially the Big 5, or Five Factor Model of personality)
- The five love languages
- Attachment theory
- 1-2-3 Magic (for when you have little kids)
- How to say "thank you" the right way

And uber-skills that apply to all areas of my life include:
- Time/energy management
- Goal setting (of course!)
- Psychology of persuasion
- How to learn (quickly)
- How to make decisions

QUOTE

"Once you realize that you have identified a passion, invest in yourself. Figure out what you need to know, what kind of experience and expertise you need to develop to do the things that you feel in your heart you will enjoy and that will sustain you both mentally and economically."
–Martha Stewart

Takeaway

Without any knowledge of your goal area, you are destined to fail; the more you "level up" your ability in your goal area, the more likely you are to succeed.

After you've set a Big Specific Goal, take time to consider the following:
- What are some subordinate "learning goals" that could support the primary goal?
- What topics should you learn about related to this goal?

- What skills should you develop related to this goal?
- How specifically will you go about gaining the knowledge and skills you need?

POWER TWEETS FOR MOTIVATION

"Embrace the journey of life-long learning! Each day offers new opportunities to grow, expand your knowledge, and sharpen your skills. Fuel your curiosity and watch your world transform! #LifeLongLearner #KnowledgeIsPower"

"Become a master of your craft by dedicating yourself to continuous learning. The pursuit of knowledge and skills not only elevates your personal growth, but also inspires others to follow your lead. #NeverStopLearning #MasterYourCraft"

"Unlock your full potential by committing to life-long learning. Every new skill and piece of knowledge you acquire paves the way to success and personal fulfillment. Invest in yourself and reap the rewards! #LifeLongLearning #InvestInYou"

"Expand your horizons through life-long learning! By constantly seeking new knowledge and experiences, you become a well-rounded individual who's adaptable, resourceful, and ready to conquer any challenge. #AlwaysLearning #EmbraceTheJourney"

"Life-long learning is the secret ingredient to a fulfilling and successful life. Embrace the excitement of discovery, nurture your curiosity, and stay open to new ideas. Keep learning, keep growing, keep thriving! #LifeLongLearner #CuriosityFuelsGrowth"

SECRET #7

Increase your ability (i.e., knowledge and skill) to maximize goal success.

HOW MIGHT YOU APPLY THIS?

- **NETWORK MARKETING**: To increase the number of people in your downline, consider enrolling in a persuasive communication course to refine your interpersonal skills, enabling you to effectively convey the benefits of your products and the advantages of joining your network marketing team to potential recruits. Additionally, stay up-to-date with the latest digital marketing strategies, such as social media advertising and content creation, to broaden your reach and attract a wider audience interested in your offerings.

- **SALES PROFESSIONAL**: To increase the number of demos you line up each week, consider attending a sales training program that focuses on cold-calling techniques and email outreach strategies, which will help you improve your approach and effectively engage prospects. Additionally, invest time in mastering your product knowledge and understanding your target market, which will allow you to tailor your pitch to demonstrate value and create a sense of urgency for potential clients.

- **MANAGER / LEADER**: To improve your team's employee engagement scores, consider participating in a leadership development program that focuses on fostering a positive work environment, effective communication, and building trust within your team. Additionally, learn about best practices for employee recognition and motivation, and implement strategies such as regular feedback sessions, team-building activities, and personalized incentives to encourage a more engaged and committed workforce.

- **CREATIVE ENTREPRENEUR**: To grow your following on TikTok, study its algorithm and trends, as well as successful creators in your niche, to gain insights into content formats and posting schedules that resonate with users and drive growth on the platform.

- **INDIVIDUAL HEALTH**: To successfully lose weight (as just one example), consider attending a nutrition workshop or consulting with a registered dietitian to learn about creating a balanced and sustainable meal plan tailored to your needs and preferences. Additionally, experience and learn about different types of physical activities, such as yoga, HIIT, or swimming, to find a workout routine you enjoy.

- **ATHLETE**: To maximize your playing minutes as a professional basketball player (for example), consider working with a specialized coach or trainer to identify areas for improvement, and sharpen your skills in areas such as ball handling, shooting, and defense. Study game footage of elite players in your position to gain insights into their techniques and decision-making, which will help you enhance your on-court performance and increase your value to your team.

- **SPOUSE OR PARENT**: To maintain a close, trusting relationship with your teenage children, consider reading books on active listening. Learn about their various interests in music, sports, or even social media. This can help to create a strong bond and demonstrate your genuine interest and support.

- **STUDENT**: To achieve a high GPA and get into a top college, consider learning study techniques such as the Pomodoro Technique or spaced repetition, and seek out supplementary educational resources like tutoring or online courses to strengthen your understanding of challenging subjects.

Self-Coaching Or Book Club Questions

1. Do you enjoy learning? Are you naturally curious about things?
2. Do you have a growth mindset? Are you patient as you strive to learn difficult things?
3. How has your knowledge contributed to goal achievement in the past?
4. How has your lack of knowledge in a particular area prevented you from achieving your goal?
5. How do you like to learn new things (e.g., books, videos, podcasts, coaches)?

SECRET 8

The Friction Formula

Engineer Your Environment For Better Behaviors

"THERE'S JUST ONE WAY TO RADICALLY CHANGE YOUR BEHAVIOR: RADICALLY CHANGE YOUR ENVIRONMENT." –BJ FOGG, PH.D.

"BEHAVIOR IS THE MIRROR IN WHICH EVERYONE SHOWS THEIR IMAGE." –JOHANN GOETHE

---

en·vi·ron·ment

The circumstances, objects, or conditions by which one is surrounded.

Remember, Dr. Locke and Dr. Latham identified four moderators that strengthen or weaken the power of goals: feedback, commitment, ability, and situation.

In this chapter, we'll focus on situation which includes your environment.

QUOTE

Goal-directed action may be facilitated or hindered by environmental factors....." –Dr. Edwin Locke

---

Your Situation *Can* Limit You

Walt Disney famously said, "If you can dream it, you can do it."

Bullsh*t.

Sure, it's a nice pep talk, but taken literally it's just complete nonsense.

If you are a serial killer in prison, serving a dozen consecutive life sentences, it is highly unlikely you'll achieve your dream of becoming an astronaut.

If you are five feet tall and 55 years old, it is highly unlikely that you will achieve your goal of becoming an NBA basketball player. (Note that the shortest NBA player ever, Muggsy Bogues, was 5' 3", and the oldest player, Nat Hickey, played his last game two days short of his 46th birthday.)

So it's true that your circumstances can limit you, but of course, most people use their circumstances as an excuse to dream small dreams or never to pursue their dreams at all.

There are plenty of inspirational stories of people overcoming situational obstacles to achieve their dreams:

- Jamaica National Bobsled Team competes in the Olympics despite the fact that there is no snow in Jamaica
- Angela Alvarez won a best new artist Grammy nomination in 2022, even though she's a 95-year-old grandma
- Erik Weihenmayer reached the peak of Mt. Everest in 2001, despite being blind
- One of the greatest filmmakers of all time, Stephen Spielberg, was rejected by USC film school twice

Add Friction, Anchor, or Relocate

The more relevant point when it comes to goal setting is that your situation—specifically your environment—is a major influence on your behaviors. This means if you can alter your environment, you'll increase your odds of success.

The simple way to think about this is:

1. Make the actions you want to do easier to do (reduce the amount of friction to do the action)
2. Make the actions you don't want to do harder to do (increase the amount of friction to do them)

Another key idea in this area is to attach a new habit to an old habit (i.e., an anchor habit). I've personally changed my environment in all of these ways:

- I put all of my vitamins in a basket next to my coffee pot because I never forget to drink coffee in the morning! (health goals)
- I put my sneakers and workout clothes right next to my bed, so I'll immediately put them on when I wake up in the morning (health goals)
- I've placed my smartphone in the bathroom, so I don't snooze the alarm when I'm trying to get up early (for health and/or writing goals)
- I moved the Facebook app icon onto the last screen of my smartphone and moved the Kindle and Substack apps to the first screen (to reduce unproductive procrastination and promote learning)
- I don't buy junk food unless my kids are home, and then I put it in the back cupboard while moving fruit and almonds to the kitchen island (health goals)
- I moved the scale in the bathroom right next to the shower door, so I'll have to step over it if I don't step on it! (health goals)
- I wear an Apple watch in the day and an Oura ring at night for frictionless sleep tracking, steps, and heart rate tracking. (health goals)
- I put books on the coffee table next to the remote so I have an equal chance of reading versus watching TV (learning goals)
- I leave a MacBook Air on my coffee table, so I'll have an equal chance of writing something rather than reading or watching TV (work goal)

RESEARCH: Move the Cookies

To reduce consumption of unhealthy foods among college students, researchers at the University of New Hampshire conducted a simple experiment. They moved the cookies in the dining hall from a main meal section in plain site, to the corner of the room. Cookie consumption dropped 14%! (Rubini, Loris and Ozabaci, Deniz, Hide the Cookie Jar)

My personal examples of shaping my environment involve my immediate surroundings, but even your macro environment can have an impact on your goals.

- Suppose you have a career goal to be an engineer working at a major tech company. Would the chances for success be better living in Montgomery, Alabama, or Silicon Valley, California?
- If your goal is to find a nature-loving, weekend-hiker soul mate, should you live in Newark, NJ, or Boulder, Colorado?
- If your goal is to become an actor, would you have more opportunities in Hollywood, California, or Detroit, Michigan?

RESEARCH: Replace Your Plates

Numerous studies have shown that we choose smaller portions when our plates are smaller. Not only that, but we feel just as full! It has to do with the Delbeouf illusion – a visual illusion based on the perceived size of one object related to another. Environment changes behaviors effortlessly!

Takeaway

Your situation—your environment—has an impact on your behaviors, which naturally impacts progress towards your goals. After you've set a challenging and specific goal, take time to consider the following:

- What are the ways I might sabotage myself?
- What will cause me not to do what I plan to do?
- How am I likely to procrastinate?
- How can I add friction to all the counterproductive things I might do?
- How can I remove friction (i.e., make it easier) related to the actions that will lead to goal success?

POWER TWEETS FOR MOTIVATION

"Create an environment that nurtures positive habits! Surround yourself with inspiration and support, making it easy to stay focused and committed. Remember, your environment shapes your destiny! #PositiveEnvironment #HabitShapers"

"Add friction to break negative habits! Re-organize your space, eliminate distractions, and make it harder to indulge in old patterns. Small changes in your environment lead to big transformations! #BreakBadHabits #AddFriction"

"Your environment is a reflection of your mindset. Cultivate a space that fosters growth, positivity, and motivation. As you shape your surroundings, you shape your habits and ultimately, your future! #PositiveSpace #HabitChange"

"Declutter your life to make way for positive habits! Clearing physical and mental clutter paves the way for healthier routines and increased productivity. Embrace the power of a supportive environment! #DeclutterForSuccess #PositiveHabits"

"Unlock the secret to lasting habit change: a supportive environment! Set up your space to encourage positive behaviors and discourage negative ones. Let your environment be your guide on the path to self-improvement! #EnvironmentMatters #HabitSuccess"

SECRET #8

Your environment is a major factor for goal success; reduce friction to maximize positive actions and increase friction to minimize negative actions.

HOW MIGHT YOU APPLY THIS?

- **NETWORK MARKETING**: To facilitate recruiting new people and growing your downline, modify your physical environment by creating a dedicated home office or workspace that is organized and comfortable. Display motivational quotes, vision boards, or success stories from your company. Have a ring light always mounted on your monitor to make creating video content easy.

- **SALES PROFESSIONAL**: To land new accounts and increase your sales, modify your environment by setting up a dedicated workspace with an ergonomic setup, ensuring you have a comfortable and efficient space for conducting calls, virtual meetings, and product demonstrations. Additionally, consider using a second monitor to easily reference product information, client data, and sales scripts during conversations, and keep a whiteboard or visual tracking system to monitor your sales targets, progress, and new account opportunities.

- **MANAGER / LEADER**: To build strong employee engagement on your team, modify your environment by creating a collaborative and inclusive workspace, with comfortable seating arrangements that encourage interaction and communication among team members. Additionally, designate a common area for displaying team goals, accomplishments, and recognition, as well as providing resources like whiteboards or pinboards for brainstorming and sharing ideas, fostering a sense of shared purpose and collective success within your team.

- **CREATIVE ENTREPRENEUR**: To attract new clients as an online fitness coach, modify your environment by creating a visually appealing and well-equipped home workout space that showcases your professionalism and expertise, which can serve as the backdrop for your live sessions, promotional photos, and video content. Additionally, set up a dedicated workspace with a reliable computer and high-speed internet connection, ensuring seamless communication with potential clients and enabling efficient management of your marketing efforts and client scheduling.

- **INDIVIDUAL HEALTH**: To help achieve your goal of losing 10% of your body weight, modify your environment by keeping your kitchen stocked with nutritious, portion-controlled meals and snacks, while removing unhealthy temptations. Additionally, create a dedicated workout space at home with essential fitness equipment, like resistance bands or a yoga mat, to encourage regular physical activity and make it easier to incorporate exercise into your daily routine.

- **ATHLETE**: To maximize your performance as a an athlete, modify your environment by creating a well-equipped home training area tailored to your sport, allowing you to consistently work on your skills and conditioning outside of team practices. Stock your kitchen with healthy foods and eliminate food and alcohol that don't support your goals.

- **SPOUSE OR PARENT**: To maintain a strong emotional connection with your spouse, modify your environment by creating comfortable and inviting shared spaces, such as a cozy living room or outdoor seating area, where you can spend quality time together, engage in meaningful conversations, or enjoy shared hobbies. Additionally, ensure your bedroom is a calm and relaxing sanctuary, free of distractions like electronic devices, to promote open communication, and intimacy.

- **STUDENT**: To achieve good grades as a high school student, modify your environment by creating a dedicated, organized, and distraction-free study space with a comfortable chair, proper lighting, and essential supplies such as textbooks, notebooks, and pens and pencils. Additionally, minimize digital distractions by silencing your phone or using website blockers during study sessions, and consider using a study timer or calendar to help manage your time effectively and maintain focus on your academic tasks.

Self-Coaching Or Book Club Questions

1. What bad habits would you like to break?
2. What triggers or situational factors tend to reinforce this bad habit, and how can you proactively avoid or overcome them?
3. What new habits would help you to reach your goal?
4. How has your existing environment helped or hurt your previous efforts to achieve your goals?

The Time Travel Cure for Procrastination

How to Defeat Your Inner Enemy

"WE ARE SO SCARED OF BEING JUDGED THAT WE LOOK FOR EVERY EXCUSE TO PROCRASTINATE." –ERICA JONG

"WE ALL SORELY COMPLAIN OF THE SHORTNESS OF TIME, AND YET HAVE MUCH MORE THAN WE KNOW WHAT TO DO WITH. OUR LIVES ARE EITHER SPENT IN DOING NOTHING AT ALL, OR IN DOING NOTHING TO THE PURPOSE, OR IN DOING NOTHING THAT WE OUGHT TO DO. WE ARE ALWAYS COMPLAINING THAT OUR DAYS ARE FEW, AND ACTING AS THOUGH THERE WOULD BE NO END OF THEM." –SENECA

---

pro·cras·ti·nate

To put off intentionally and habitually.

Why do many people derail from their goal path while others seem to achieve their goals time and again?

Why do we decide and act in certain ways today, only to decide something totally different tomorrow (and often all the tomorrows after that)?

QUOTE

"Everyone procrastinates, but not everyone is a procrastinator. Procrastination is an issue of self-regulation failure, and specifically misregulation of emotional states, not a time management problem as often presumed." **–Dr. Joseph Ferrari**

What Does My Rowing Machine, Fine Literature, and Iceberg Lettuce All Have In Common?

Here are some examples of procrastination from my own life.

- I routinely buy serious novels and history books to expand my horizons, but they remain unclicked in Kindle or Audible.
- For many months, I've had several documentaries in my Netflix My List but keep leapfrogging them with the Trending Now shows.
- I spent $3,000 on an Ergatta Rower and have used it three times in a year.
- Every Sunday, I buy tons of lettuce and vegetables for salads and inevitably throw the rotting gooey mess out a week later.

I'm guilty of all those things and so much more. (Get in touch if you want a good deal on a hydro rower!)

If you can't relate to my little flaws in behavior, perhaps these items resonate with you.

- Leaving dirty dishes in the sink overnight?
- Cramming all night before a test?
- Delaying difficult conversations at home or at work?

Why do we routinely procrastinate—put off—the actions that we know will lead us closer to our goal?

The answer is a little deep, but if you hang with me, this chapter (more than any other) has the power to completely blow the lid off your life (in a good way).

RESEARCH

20% of people are chronic procrastinators, according to Dr. Ferrari and confirmed in dozens of studies around the world. Note that several studies suggest this number is higher among people who have Attention-Deficit / Hyperactivity Disorder (ADHD).

We Think Of Our Future Selves As Strangers

The answer is that your present self and your future self are two different people; your future self is a stranger to you.

Sounds freaky, doesn't it?

As reported in Nautilus, New York University professor, Hal Hershfield, took fMRI images of peoples' brains as they were thinking of themselves and their future selves. Brain imaging showed that when people thought about themselves in the future, the part of the brain that thinks of other people lit up.

Their future self "felt" like somebody else. In fact, their neural activity when they described themselves in a decade was the same neural activity that lit up when they described Matt Damon or Natalie Portman.

In other words, our neural activity and emotions treat our future-self like a stranger.

KEY POINT

Your brain treats your "future self" as if they are a stranger.

Why is this so important?

Because "we" (our present selves) like to feel good now, we don't mind making that future stranger person take all the pain.

- "Would you like that new pair of shoes right now? That stranger in the future will pay the credit card." Sure, let's have some fun!
- "Would you like to go out with your friends tonight? That stranger can just double up the study time tomorrow." It's party time!
- "Would you like to eat pizza, a cheeseburger, fries, and ice cream for dinner? It's that future stranger who will look flabby and get a heart attack." You had me at Pizza! How about meat lovers deluxe?

Scientists prove this theory time and again:

- When Hershfield asked people how many minutes they'd volunteer to tutor students, those who thought they would have to do it today offered up far fewer minutes than those students who were making a commitment to do it next semester.
- Princeton psychologist, Emily Pronin, did an experiment where she told people they had to consume a nasty ketchup-soy sauce drink on behalf of science. She asked them how much they'd be willing to drink. Those who thought they had to drink it right away promised to consume two tablespoons full. Those who were told they didn't have to do it until later said they (their future self) would consume half a cup.

It wouldn't be a problem if our future-self actually did do all the things we want them to do. If they did cut back on spending to pay off the credit card debt. If they did double up on study hours. If they did get on that expensive rowing machine.

But they don't, because when tomorrow arrives—when it's the present—you're back to being "you," your present self, once again saying, "I'm going to do what I feel like now, and let that future stranger do what's right tomorrow." It never ends. The future never arrives; you're always in the present.

How To Overcome Present Bias With Time Travel

So how can we overcome this present bias we have?

How can we make sure we aren't putting the pain or effort always onto our future-self-stranger who never actually arrives to do the heavy lifting?

The secret is to time travel, and you "travel into the future" by thinking instead of just doing or reacting to your feelings.

You need to get in the habit of pausing, projecting into (thinking of) the future, and realizing that your future self is your enemy. Let me repeat it. Many people say you need to befriend your future selves, treat them with understanding and kindness, and come to terms with them. I say the opposite: your future self is the enemy.

Your future self is trying hard to sabotage your Big Dream, trying to trick you into not doing what you know you should be doing today–right now. And if you think about your future self in this way, you are more likely to fight back.

If you could listen to the self-talk inside my head (a very scary proposition indeed), it might sound like this on some mornings when I just don't feel like it:

Ugh, it's 6:00 am, and I'm supposed to hop on the treadmill. God, I'm so tired...shouldn't have stayed up late watching Dirty Dancing for the 20th time...and I've got that call with my boss at 9:00. It's kind of rushing it. Maybe I'll just coffee up, prep for my meeting, and hit the treadmill tonight after work...yeah, I'll be more awake then, probably get a better workout, won't be rushed, and can actually spend more time on the treadmill if I do it tonight instead...[insert sound of record scratch] WHOA, WHOA, WHOA! WAIT JUST A MINUTE! I see what's going on here...I'm trusting my future-tonight-self to hop on this dang treadmill. I don't trust that dude one bit. He's going to sabotage me. Of course, it's logical now, to put this off until tonight. But, my future self is an untrustworthy jerk who is going to whine like a little baby, "I came home late, I'm so tired, I'm hungry, what's missing one workout anyway, I'm on track with my big plan so it doesn't really matter, I can just do double the miles tomorrow...." I'm not going to let that future loser derail me. RIGHT

NOW, I can only trust myself to do what's right. It ain't gonna be pretty, but treadmill, here I come!

Your New Mantra

I can only trust myself, RIGHT NOW,
to do what's right.

The first step to prevent derailing is to catch yourself—your inner monologue—and realize that the future self won't do what you want them to do.

The second way to utilize time travel is to proactively think about how your future self will sabotage you and fight them in the present.

For example, tomorrow I'm going to eat right. I'm going to eat the right foods in the right portions. I'm motivated! Hmm, how will my future self-sabotage this plan? Well, I bet they'll feel really hungry and then just grab the giant bag of potato chips and scarf them down. I bet they'll be too tired to make a healthy dinner and will just Door Dash a pizza instead. OK, so how can I fight them? How can I prevent that? Aha! I'll food prep all of my meals for tomorrow—heck, for the whole week—right now. That way, they take no time to just microwave and eat. Doesn't matter how hungry or busy or tired your future self is; it will actually be easier just to eat a healthy meal than something else.

KEY POINT

The future will be no less busy than today.

Another example: tomorrow, I will get up at five before anyone else in the house is awake, and I will work on my novel for a full hour. Day by day, and in a year, I'll have finished my first novel! Oh, oh, but how will future self sabotage me? They'll probably shut off the alarm and go back to sleep. Or snooze it five times. OK, so how do I fight that? How do I prevent that? Aha! I'm literally going to put my phone in the bathroom, and I'll pick a really obnoxious sound for the alarm. That way, to shut it off, I'll have to get out of bed and walk into the bathroom to do it. At that point, I'm sure I'll just splash water on my face and not return to bed. Bonus idea! I'll have the coffee pot scheduled to brew a pot at 4:55. By the time I wake up, the smell of coffee will motivate me, and I can get the caffeine pumping in my veins as soon as possible.

The key thing is to train your brain to stop in the middle of your derailing thoughts—your self-sabotaging thoughts—and project out to your future self and realize that that person will be no less busy, and no more motivated than your present self.

POWER TWEETS FOR MOTIVATION

"Procrastination is the thief of time! Conquer it by breaking tasks into smaller steps and tackling them one by one. Remember, progress today leads to success tomorrow. Start now! #OvercomeProcrastination #DefeatPresentBias"

"Focus on the long-term rewards! Defeat present bias by visualizing the future benefits of your actions. Stay disciplined and committed to your goals and reap the fruits of your hard work! #BeatProcrastination #FutureFocused"

"Seize the day and overcome procrastination! Prioritize your tasks, set deadlines, and hold yourself accountable. Transform your intentions into actions and make each day count. #NoMoreProcrastination #CarpeDiem"

"Ignite your motivation and say goodbye to procrastination! Keep your goals front and center, reminding yourself of the reasons behind your actions. Let your passion propel you forward! #DefeatProcrastination #StayMotivated"

> *"Build a bridge between your present self and future success! Overcome procrastination by recognizing the long-term impact of your daily actions. Stay focused, work hard, and make your future self proud! #NoProcrastination #BridgeToSuccess"*

SECRET #9

Only trust your present self to do what's right; plan now to defeat your sabotaging future self.

HOW MIGHT YOU APPLY THIS?

- **NETWORK MARKETING**: To defeat procrastination and ensure you consistently post to social media and engage with your followers, start by creating a content calendar outlining the topics and post types for each day, which will help you stay organized and focused. Schedule specific time slots daily for content creation, posting, and engaging with your audience, treating these tasks as non-negotiable appointments. Set reminders or alarms on your phone to hold yourself accountable.

- **SALES PROFESSIONAL**: To defeat your future self, who might sabotage your efforts to prospect and network online, schedule an hour of prospecting for the first hour of your work day. Leave your computer on and open LinkedIn so it's the first thing you see. Put your phone on airplane mode during prospecting time so you don't get distracted by messages or emails.

- **MANAGER / LEADER**: Holding weekly or bi-weekly one-on-one meetings with your team members is a significant driver of employee engagement—and often never happens because there are always deadlines and fires to put out. Overcome self-sabotage by scheduling recurring "O3" meetings every week on the same day and time. Hold them as early in the day as possible before things get hectic. Once they begin, silence your phone and messaging apps so you remain focused on the conversation.

- **CREATIVE ENTREPRENEUR**: To defeat your self-sabotaging future self, schedule your digital content creation for the first hour of your day before "life happens" and while your energy is high. Leave a sticky note on your monitor that says, "Done is better than perfect!" Have your ring light, camera, and other production equipment already set up and ready to go.

- **INDIVIDUAL HEALTH**: To defeat procrastination and ensure you take the right actions tomorrow to lose 5 pounds, schedule your workouts and meal planning/preparation into your calendar, treating them as non-negotiable appointments, and consider setting reminders or alarms to hold yourself accountable for these tasks, making it more likely that you'll follow through and develop healthier habits.

- **ATHLETE**: Are you a student athlete who spends too much time gaming and not enough time studying or going to class? Consider giving your game console to a friend to hold onto until after your mid-terms. Use an app that blocks social media and websites during study times. Get yourself into a quiet place without distractions during study times.

- **SPOUSE OR PARENT**: You want to do something great for your spouse's upcoming birthday but are "crazy busy." Defeat your procrastinating future-self by brainstorming gift ideas far in advance. Add a note on your calendar to buy it, leaving plenty of time for shipping or inventory problems. Schedule another task on your calendar for the restaurant reservation so you can get the time slot you want.

- **STUDENT**: To ensure you finish a school report by Friday (for example), start by breaking the project down into smaller, more manageable tasks, such as outlining, researching, and writing. Schedule specific time slots in your calendar for each task. Declutter your desk and remove all distractions, such as your phone or social media. Tell your friends and family ahead of time that you have to grind this week so they'll leave you alone.

Self-Coaching Or Book Club Questions

1. How have you derailed your goal progress in the past?
2. In what ways have you procrastinated in the past week?
3. Do you typically do what you feel like doing? Or do you do what you are committed to doing?
4. What can you do today to ensure your future self doesn't sabotage you tomorrow?

Three to Thrive

How Many Goals Will Give You The Best Possible Life?

"YOU CAN HAVE ANYTHING YOU WANT... BUT NOT EVERYTHING YOU WANT." –SUSAN FUSSELL

"THE MAN WHO CHASES TWO RABBITS CATCHES NEITHER." – CONFUCIUS

---

bal·ance

Equipoise between contrasting, opposing, or interacting elements; mental and emotional steadiness.

How many goals should you have?

The correct answer is three.

OK, OK, it's not that easy. That's my answer, but yours might be different.

There are a lot of different opinions on this, and my own view is that each additional goal dilutes the power and focus of the others. If you have just one goal, all your focus and attention will be on that one achievement.

If you have two goals, by definition, you'll be splitting your focus and attention, and passion between them. If you have three...

KEY POINT

Each additional goal dilutes the power and focus of the others.

And yet, many people disagree with my simple answer: three.

Tony Robbins Says Four

In his book, *Awaken the Giant Within*, Tony Robbins suggests that to have a balanced life, you should set goals in four different areas:

- Personal goals
- Career or business goals
- Toys or adventure goals
- Contribution or ways to give back goals

The Five F's

Another popular framework is known as the five F's:

- Faith
- Family
- Friends
- Fitness
- Finances

Zig Ziglar Said Seven

Motivational giant, Zig Ziglar, suggests seven areas to set goals:

- Financial
- Spiritual
- Physical
- Intellectual
- Family
- Social
- Career

Daymond John Says Ten!

Daymond John is a self-made multi-millionaire, founder of FUBU, and a "Shark" on the TV show, Shark Tank. During his media tour to promote his book, *Powershift*, he often spoke of the power of goal setting.

Specifically, John said he always has a set of 10 goals.

- Six goals that expire in six months
- One goal that expires in two years
- One goal that expires in five years
- One goal that expires in ten years
- One goal that expires in 20 years

"I read my goals every single morning and every single night before I go to sleep, because it's the last thing I want to think about and I want to dream about," John says.

Storytime: Tyler Is A Self-Made Millionaire (And His Kids Aren't Speaking To Him)

Most people who see my friend Tyler would say he's got it all. They envy his life. Tyler is a VP of Sales, makes $500,000 a year, made millions from exercising stock options, wears Armani suits, drives a Mercedes SL 500, season tickets to the Eagles on the 50-yard line, Diamond Club for Phillies, his home is 5,000 square feet (pool, of course), plus a shore house and an apartment in Manhattan. Oh, and a smoking hot wife and two beautiful young boys with mops of blond hair.

But Tyler's close friends and colleagues also know...he's only home to see his kids two or three nights a month. He feels tremendous financial pressure; even though he makes a lot, he spends a lot. Sometimes he even gets in trouble with the IRS for not paying his taxes on time, and worse, he's lost tens of thousands of dollars gambling. Tyler drinks Scotch at night. A lot. He cheats on his wife when he's on the road. A lot.

I've known Tyler for over 20 years and have seen his life's later chapters. Multiple divorces. One son won't talk to him, and the other merely tolerates him. He has no true friends—spends his time with people who report to him at work. Lots of extra pounds from too much wining and dining...high cholesterol, high blood pressure, trouble sleeping. Just another chubby, lonely, middle-aged millionaire.

Why I Focus On "Three to Thrive"

Tyler isn't actually a real person. Unfortunately, he's an amalgamation of a dozen Tylers I know. My professional speaker friends are at the top of their game but traveling away from their families 200+ days a year. My CEO friends work 80-100 hours a week. Hustle, hustle, hustle. There are very, very few self-made millionaires I know who have a great family life.

Even when I was young and dumb and chasing the hard dollar, I knew I never wanted to achieve financial success at the expense of my children. Having "only" five or ten million dollars and a great relationship with my kids was going to be better than $100 million and no relationship with my kids.

So early on, my goals were focused on (1) money and (2) time spent with my family. And that was pretty much it for almost two decades. And because goals work like magic, I made a lot of money, and my kids turned out pretty great, and I probably spent more time with my kids than any Dad I know. But...

Looking back, the big thing I omitted was my own health. The nights where I'd spend time with my kids and tuck them into bed, and then I'd work without going to sleep myself for the rest of the night. I never exercised. Nutrition? I'd grab a coffee and buttered roll from the quick mart for breakfast. Two slices of pizza at my desk for lunch. Pig out on junk food when I got home and ate a late dinner, usually pasta or some other carb-goodness. I was sick all the time, completely exhausted, and usually depressed.

But I was in my twenties and thirties and sort of got away with it. But it was a mistake. I'm still fighting to get into fighting shape, and now realize that eating healthy and working out doesn't take a lot of time and will give you more energy and clarity of thought, which will actually make you more successful faster.

So, my big three are family, health, and wealth.

"THREE TO THRIVE"

Health – Wealth – Relationships

But What About Those Other Things?

You might wonder, "What about those other Zig Ziglar areas like Social? Don't you want to give back to the world? Are you starving yourself spiritually?"

No, not at all. I'm a huge believer in giving back. With my annual tithing, I've built over a dozen libraries for kids in Asia, donated to local health clinics, supported a local church and a distant Zen monastery, and spent a lot of time on non-profit boards. But it's something I just do. I don't set a goal around it.

Similarly, when it comes to spirituality, I read various religious texts every morning and meditate (but not consistently, yet). Again, I don't make a goal for these things, they are just things I incorporate into my life.

I'm not saying health, wealth, and family should be your areas of goal setting–though it's a good place to start. Maybe you should only have one thing. Maybe you should have five things.

The critical truth is that the more goals you have, the more you dilute the "magic" in each of them. So choose wisely, my friend.

POWER TWEETS FOR MOTIVATION

"Find balance and fulfillment by setting goals in various areas of your life! Nurture your mind, body, and soul by focusing on personal, professional, and social growth. Embrace the harmony of a well-rounded life! #BalancedGoals #LifeInHarmony"

"Diversify your goals for a richer, more fulfilling life! Cultivate health, relationships, career, and personal growth to experience the full spectrum of happiness and success. #BalancedLife #FulfillmentInDiversity"

"Achieve true success by pursuing goals in all dimensions of life! Balance professional ambition with personal growth, strong relationships, and self-care. Be the best version of yourself in every aspect! #WellRoundedGoals #LifeSuccess"

"Create a life masterpiece by setting goals across multiple domains! Just as colors blend to form a beautiful landscape, a balanced approach to goal setting leads to a fulfilling and meaningful life. #LifeBalance #GoalSettingArt"

"Life is a carousel of opportunities! Set goals in various areas to ensure a fulfilling ride. As you nurture each aspect of your life, you'll discover new strengths, passions, and joys. #BalancedGoals #FulfillingLife"

SECRET #10

Too few goals will lead to an unbalanced life; too many will reduce the odds of success for all of them.

HOW MIGHT YOU APPLY THIS?

For your life, you might consider setting big goals for health, wealth, and relationships. And you may also want to consider off-setting goals within each area. For example...

- **NETWORK MARKETING**: How can you balance your goals for recruiting new members to your team while coaching and supporting existing members?
- **SALES PROFESSIONAL**: How can you balance prospecting for new accounts with expanding business at existing accounts?
- **MANAGER / LEADER**: How can you balance company KPIs with team engagement?
- **CREATIVE ENTREPRENEUR**: How can you balance creating new content with engaging with team members?
- **INDIVIDUAL HEALTH**: How can you balance physical health with mental health?
- **ATHLETE**: How can you balance individual success with team success?
- **SPOUSE OR PARENT**: How can you care for your children while also practicing self-care?
- **STUDENT**: How can you strive for a high GPA while maintaining healthy relationships and mental health?

Self-Coaching Or Book Club Questions

The challenge is that you don't want to have too few goals and thus an unbalanced life, but you also don't want too many goals, which will dilute your ability to achieve them.

1. What areas of your life are most important to you?
2. Which of these areas do you naturally satisfy without the use of goals?
3. Which areas of might require stronger goal power for you to achieve them?
4. Think about your list of goals and consider, if you achieve only these goals, will that be OK with you? In other words, will you feel fulfilled and have no regrets about your life?

Destroy This Book

What If There Was A Better Way?

"I HOPE EVERYBODY COULD GET RICH AND FAMOUS AND WILL HAVE
EVERYTHING THEY EVER DREAMED OF, SO THEY WILL KNOW THAT
IT'S NOT THE ANSWER." –JIM CARREY

"YOU ARE IMPERFECT, YOU ARE WIRED FOR STRUGGLE, BUT YOU
ARE WORTHY OF LOVE AND BELONGING." –BRENÉ BROWN

I have a confession: I don't set goals anymore. At least not like I just
described in this book. For the first fifty years of my life, I thought they
served me well, but now I'm not so sure.

Yes, goals are powerful.

And they may hurt us far more than they help us.

And you already hit the lottery. You already have everything you'll ever
need.

Goal Setting and the Delay of Happiness

There are two fundamental problems with goal setting: they can limit
potential and be bad for mental health.

Regarding potential, it's the very real danger of setting your goals far too
low or sticking with a path for too long when there is a better destination–

maybe even easier to get to—if you'd just be willing to look up and be open to new possibilities.

But the more significant problem is that goals can play into our insecurities and propagate a sense of dissatisfaction. Tying our self-esteem to goal attainment can trigger a damaging cycle where we're perpetually awaiting happiness in some distant future achievement rather than finding joy in the present.

The pursuit of goals often fuels a persistent sense of dissatisfaction. As we meet one objective, we set our sights on another, creating an infinite loop where fulfillment is always tantalizingly just out of reach. This can instill a sense of futility like we're on a never-ending treadmill of aspiration. Inevitably leading to stress, anxiety, and possibly burnout.

RESEARCH

30% of all entrepreneurs experience depression, according to a study by Dr. Michael Freeman, a clinical professor at the University of California, San Francisco.

Chasing My Wealth Goals Into Oblivion

There's a joke that I and a lot of other writers say, "I hate writing. But I love having written."

That sentiment is pretty much how I feel about my goals. "I hate having goals. But I like achieving them." But the sad thing is, even that last part isn't exactly true.

When it comes to wealth and career success, I've shared how I went from a broke-as-a-joke lower-middle-class kid to selling my company for over a million dollars at age 30. I had that single goal to become a millionaire, which gave it power. And it came to be. But at a huge toll.

For the five years I was chasing the goal, every minute I wasn't working toward the goal felt wasted. Mowing the lawn? I was angry. The wife wants me to visit her parents all day Sunday? I was miserable. Out on date night? I was thinking about the sales call worth $100,000 that was scheduled for the next day. Fitness? I was skinny fat. Nutrition? Don't eat at all or eat what was fast (think pizza, pasta, bagels). I'm stoic by nature and nurture, so looking from the outside, nobody had a clue of my true condition. I was physically and mentally ill.

And when I achieved the goal—when I sold my company for almost $2 million—what happened? I set a bigger financial goal and repeated the process. When I sold that company five years later, I set a new goal and did it again.

Three successful business exits in 15 years—my goals were achieved. And then what? Well, I got divorced within a year. Instantly lost over half the money I had pursued for over a decade. And literally—not metaphorically—I woke up one morning without a job, company, or wife and kids in the house and thought, "Why should I get out of bed? What am I supposed to do?"

I felt alone and empty.

Chasing My Health Goals Into Misery

As I'm writing this sentence, I've just finished a four-month-long weight loss "cut." On January 1, after my weight reached an all-time high and I strayed into the clinical definition of overweight, I hired two coaches and decided enough was enough.

I set a health goal, made it my number one goal, and it worked. I lost over 10% of my body weight in about 100 days. Goals work like magic. But what was my life like during the last four months?

Well, I was eating 500 calories less each day than what is needed to maintain my body weight while also walking 10,000 - 15,000 steps and working out three to five days a week. And the calories I was consuming were carefully dialed in to make sure I was getting the right amount of protein, fats, and carbs. This means weighing food, preparing meals ahead of time, and recording everything that goes into your mouth into the MyFitnessPal app.

It was hard. The first month felt like I had the flu. My whole body ached, I was exhausted, I was hungry. How good of a partner do you think I was during this time? Do you feel like "date night" when you have the flu? And putting all those hours into health had to come from somewhere. Primarily, they came at the expense of my company, which just had the worst quarter since the pandemic.

And mentally, it wasn't like I was having fun. Every single day get on the scale and begin the morning feeling like a failure. *Crap, I only lost .2 pounds since yesterday.* Taking body photos each week and sending them to my coaches. *No difference! What the F does it take to get six-pack abs?* Doing pushups to failure, which is about ten for me, while watching a YouTube video of someone doing 100 pushups with claps, and jumping, leg swings. *I suck!*

Don't get me wrong, I actually don't regret the health goal. But I triggered that goal only because I felt my health problems had become pretty severe—I needed an intervention. And this was a short-term goal, not a multi-year goal. And as expected, achieving that goal came at a cost to all the other areas of my life.

"You're Not Normal," My Therapist Told Me

I used to love reviewing the annual Inc. 500 list of fastest-growing companies. In fact, one of my companies was even on the list for a couple of years. (This was before Inc. magazine turned it into a money grab and made it to the Inc. 5000 list.)

I would always go look at the top ten or twenty companies and look for patterns and outliers. Maybe several new companies at the top are all in the digital advertising business. Dig further and notice they are all selling leads to colleges. Hmm, good business—until the government cracked down. Maybe the top companies are all in one or two industries, and then there is an outlier. Like right now, the list from 2022 has a bunch of health services and financial services companies, but sticking out at #15 is a company called TeamBuilding.com. That's weird. Wonder what unique thing they are doing.

But I would also do another thing with the Inc. 500. I would look up the founders of each of the top companies. And often, they were people younger than me. And that made me feel bad. "Holy crap, this guy is 28 years old, and his company is doing $50 million a year. I'm 35 years old and only doing $12 million a year. I'm such a loser!" It would bum me out for a couple of days. And don't even get me started on how I feel every time I see a "30 Under 30" awards list. *Damn, I suck!*

QUOTE

"To compare is to despair." –**Anonymous**

When my marriage was busting up, we started couples therapy, which then turned into solo therapy, which then strayed into me talking about whatever was on my mind.

I told my therapist about my reaction to seeing people younger than me who were so much more successful. I can't even remember why I was on the topic, and I wasn't sharing it as something to work on. It was like incidental to whatever else we were talking about. But I remember our conversation clearly.

Therapist: That's not normal, Kevin.

Me: Huh? What do you mean?

Therapist: Seeing someone who has more than you or is at another level of success and feeling negative about it. That's not normal.

Me: Are you sure? I mean, doesn't everyone feel that way seeing someone else who is more successful than they are?

Therapist: No.

Me: (Incredulous)

Therapist: When I go to the annual conference for therapists, I see all kinds of people who are my age or younger, and many have written books, and I haven't. Or they have a big thriving practice, and I don't. Or they've won awards, and I haven't. It never makes me feel bad about myself.

Me: Are you sure?

Therapist: Maybe there is a fleeting thought like, "I bet it's nice to have more money." Or maybe, "I should think about writing a book someday." But I don't even recall having those thoughts.

It's funny to me now, but it never occurred to me that other people didn't react like I did. I mean, I still think people suffer from a lot of jealousy because of the curated lives we all see on Instagram. I know the idea of "keeping up with the Jones" isn't a new concept.

QUOTE

"Comparison is the thief of joy."
—Theodore Roosevelt

But what I learned was that I had it at a whole other level.

And many achievement-oriented, goal-oriented people like myself basically are suffering from low self-worth.

The root cause of our behavior is a deep inner fear that we are not enough. We are not worthy of acceptance or love. So what do we do? We achieve. Everyone will know I'm worthy if I make six figures a year. If I drive a Ferrari, everyone will know I'm worthy. Everyone will know I'm worthy if I make the Inc 500 list. If I have a trophy wife, everyone will know I'm worthy.

The powerful trap that lies ahead for everyone who is chasing external validation is that it's never enough. You can be a millionaire, and you'll be looking up at a bunch of people worth tens of millions. You can have $100 million, and you'll look small compared to all the billionaires. Someone will always have a bigger yacht, a better house, a hotter wife, more chiseled abs—whatever. You never truly stop chasing because there is no final end point to arrive at.

And, of course, all of this chasing is just nonsense. Our worth doesn't come from our external accomplishments. I've learned to value myself and others by other things. Are they a good person? Do they have good values? Do they treat other people well? Do they have a great connection with their spouse and kids? Do they give to charity? Are they creative? Are they happy?

You Don't Need to Set Goals To Be Wildly Successful

In this book, I've shared many stories of people who used goals to achieve incredible success. But the truth is that there are also many super-successful people who never set goals.

The most financially successful friend I have is my former partner, Rudy Karsan. I remember being somewhat frustrated when I asked him about his own goal setting process. I thought I could mine some good stories from my good friend with intimate details! But he told me he never really sets goals in his personal life. I didn't believe him, so I kept pressing. The most I got was, "Well, I kind of thought having a net worth of $100 million would be pretty cool. That seemed like a good number. But it turns out it's not a big deal."

He didn't have a specific goal that he broke down into milestones. He didn't write down his goal and read it every day. And he didn't proactively use strategies to increase his commitment.

Another friend of mine, Meido Moore, is a Zen monk. He built a new monastery, called Korinji, in Wisconsin and has written several books about Zen Buddhism. Once, I interviewed him on my podcast and asked him if he had set a goal to build the monastery. I asked if he set a goal to write a book. He laughed at me.

Moore explained that the original idea for the monastery came from his Zen teacher, and then he started talking about it to others in the Zen and Aikido groups he was part of. His explanation of how it came about is maddening to those of us stuck to the step-by-step way of manifesting things. He talks about people donating money, and eventually, they had enough to buy land. He talks about people donating their time and materials to build the monastery. As he describes it, he has an almost wonder in his voice. Like, "Wow, isn't this crazy how this came to be?"

Richard Feynman On Curiosity Over Conformity

Richard Feynman was an American physicist renowned for his work in the field of quantum electrodynamics, for which he won the Nobel Prize in 1965. Beyond his scientific accomplishments, Feynman was also known for his wit and teaching prowess—immortalized in "The Feynman Lectures on Physics."

In his book, *Surely You're Joking, Mr. Feynman!*, he recalls an incident from his art class. His teacher kept imploring him to "loosen up" to no avail. Finally, Feynman was asked to sketch without glancing at his paper, focusing solely on the model. He was surprised to find that the result was pretty good. He said he could see a "semi-Picasso-like strength" in his work.

This unexpected outcome sparked an epiphany. In his words, "I had thought that 'loosen up' meant 'make sloppy drawings,' but it really meant to relax and not worry about how the drawing is going to come out." The lesson here isn't just about art, but about embracing the process without being obsessed with the end result.

Throughout his career, Feynman was not constrained by the rigidity of goal setting, and he didn't let targets dictate his journey. For him, it was about the process, the exploration, and the learning. He said, "Study hard what interests you the most in the most undisciplined, irreverent, and original manner possible."

Elite Network Marketers Fail 8 Out of 10 Times

Earlier in this book I introduced Fabiola Barinas and Alan Rodriguez, a married couple who have reached the "Chairman's Club" level at Herbalife—the second highest level possible, which puts them into the elite .1% of all distributors. I talked about how they set very high goals, which at first seemed improbable.

In fact, they told me with a hearty laugh that they've actually failed to hit their goals in eight of the ten years. But despite these failures, they're in the top echelon of Herbalife performers. Emotionally, their goal setting was an exercise in thinking big and planning backwards. But they didn't feel stress or shame when they fell short. As Fabiola told me, "Shoot for the stars and if you miss, you've made it to the moon."

Steve Jobs Connects The Dots

Steve Jobs, of course, was the co-founder of Apple, founder of NeXT, CEO of Pixar, and noted as the driving force behind products like the iMac, iPod, iPhone, App Store, and more. But his greatest gift might actually be the 2005 commencement address he gave at Stanford.

In it, he tells the story of how he dropped out of college, but then just "dropped in" to whatever classes he was interested in, including one class on calligraphy. He describes learning about typography and typefaces and said, "None of this had even a hope of any practical application in my life. But 10 years later, when we were designing the first Macintosh computer, it all came back to me." A key driver of the success of the Mac came from his pursuit of learning for the sake of learning a decade earlier.

"You can't connect the dots looking forward," Jobs said. "You can only connect them looking backward. So you have to trust that the dots will somehow connect in your future. You have to trust in something -- your gut, destiny, life, karma, whatever. This approach has never let me down, and it has made all the difference in my life."

The Golden Buddha Worth $300 Million

Once hidden in plain sight, the Golden Buddha, known in Thai as Phra Phuttha Maha Suwana Patimakon, is a profound metaphor for the true value we all have inside and how layers of programming hide our potential and our potential for deep happiness. Here's the strange but true story.

In the mid-twentieth century, workers were moving the assumed stone statue from a dilapidated temple in Bangkok when it accidentally fell from a crane. As it hit the ground, the plaster cracked, revealing a glimmer of gold beneath. Intrigued, the workers began to chip away at the exterior, uncovering an awe-inspiring sight: a 9.8-foot-tall, 5.5-ton solid gold statue. With today's gold prices, it's worth over $300 million dollars.

Historians believe the Golden Buddha was camouflaged in the 13th or 14th century to protect it from invading armies from Burma. Its true value, hidden for centuries, was finally revealed in a twist of fate.

I think of this story often. How many of us think we have to become something or someone?

How many of us think happiness is something to discover, acquire, or become in the future?

How many of us have covered over our inherent value, our inner beauty, and our deep peace with layers of mud from family, friends, teachers, advertising, social media, and society in general?

You Have What You Need

Seeking external validation is a natural human social desire that begins in childhood, as we crave the approval of our parents and caregivers. However, excessive reliance on external validation can lead to a diminished sense of self-worth and an unhealthy need to strive for higher and higher levels of achievement.

Instead, we must strive for higher internal validation rooted in our beliefs, values, and interests. Developing strong self-reflection, self-awareness, and self-compassion can help us cultivate a sense of self-worth that is not dependent on external validation.

In his book, The Way to Love, Indian Jesuit priest Anthony De Mello discusses the differences between external and internal feelings. He suggests we contrast the feelings we experience from success or winning against the feeling we get from being totally absorbed in a job we enjoy. He suggests we contrast the feelings we get from power and popularity, with our feelings from intimacy with our partner or enjoying deep companionship with our friends.

By engaging in such exercises, it becomes evident that the satisfaction gained from external achievements is often fleeting. Long-lasting contentment, joy, and peace are more likely to be found in our work, friendships, connection with nature, and moments of contemplation.

QUOTE

"There's a science to achievement, but an art to fulfillment; and achievement without fulfillment is the ultimate failure." –Kien Vuu, MD

You Already Hit The Lottery

If you find yourself continually striving and focusing heavily on goals, take a moment to remember one crucial thing: you've already won the lottery of life. The mere fact of your existence as a human being on this Earth is nothing short of miraculous!

Consider this: the estimated probability of you being born as 'you' is about 1 in 400 trillion, based on the odds of a specific egg and a specific sperm uniting. Now, let's put that into a broader context. NASA estimates that our Milky Way galaxy alone houses a staggering 100 billion planets. Against those odds, your existence on Earth is already a 1 in 100 billion occurrences.

But let's not stop there. Earth is home to around 8.7 million distinct species. So, even if you were guaranteed to be born as a life form on Earth, the odds of you being part of the human species are 1 in 8.7 million.

So, if you're reading this, remember you've already hit the jackpot. You've beaten extraordinary odds to be given this one precious life. Do you truly require a chiseled physique or a flashy sports car to feel content? You've already won the most significant lottery there is: life itself!

KEY POINT

Focus on what you have instead of what you don't have. On what's right in your world instead of what's wrong. On where you're going instead of what you've been through.

Forward Progress: The Gain, Not The Gap

Top performers are keen on identifying the gap between where they are today and where they want to be. A herculean effort is expended trying to close that gap.

But often, that gap can feel so distant we procrastinate, or after repeated setbacks, we become demotivated and give up, or we just suffer along the way. Authors Dan Sullivan and Ben Hardy discuss this idea in their book, *The Gap and The Gain*.

Most people, especially highly ambitious people, are unhappy because of how they measure their progress. We all have an 'ideal,' a moving target that is always out of reach. When we measure ourselves against that ideal, we're in the Gap. However, when we measure ourselves against our previous selves, we're in the Gain.

When we measure our progress by our Gains rather than by the Gaps that still remain, we liberate ourselves from feelings of failure. Instead, we appreciate just how far we've come, and that positivity fuels even more progress.

A powerful question to focus on the Gain is, "Go back to the person you were one year ago. What would that person think of the progress you've made?" Spend time celebrating those wins and highlighting your personal growth.

Negative energy can fuel you in the short term, but it won't sustain you over time. Be mindful of the Gap, but celebrate how far you've come.

How To Make Goals Less Toxic

So how do we reconcile the power of goal setting with the perils of goal setting?

First, diversify your goals. My "three to thrive" are health, wealth, and relationships. Yes, each of these goals will be diluted because of the other two, but it will ensure that you live a balanced life.

Second, add people to your goals. I interviewed pastor Mark Batterson about his goal-related book, *Win the Day*, and raised the issue of the dark side of goals. He gave me great advice.

"My goals went through a radical transformation in my late 30s because almost all of them were a bit selfish. They were all about me, myself and I. And so, I started adding a relational component to my goals. So rather than setting a goal of going to the top of the Eiffel Tower, why not make the goal to kiss my wife on top of the Eiffel Tower? If I want to run a triathlon or swim the escape from Alcatraz, why don't I do that with my son or daughter?" –Mark Batterson

Three, chase goals only for critical short-term priorities. Four months ago, I made the conscious decision to set a weight loss goal because I felt the situation had gotten serious. A year of health failure without a goal, and trending into dangerous territory. So I set one goal for four months. As expected, I hit the goal, but all other areas of my life were sub-optimal. But now I can relax the health goal, and rebalance.

Four, give yourself a break from goals. My fitness coach encourages clients to enter a "maintenance" mode after a few months of weight loss. He insists on a break even if they're making good progress and have more weight to lose. This doesn't mean reverting to unhealthy habits but rather eating at a maintenance level and easing off intense workouts. This break makes the fitness journey more enjoyable and sustainable in the long run. Similarly, give yourself permission to step away from relentless striving occasionally. Take summers off, explore your interests, or pause goal setting during holiday months to be more present with your family.

In Their Own Words: Racer Phil Hanson Turns Goal Behaviors Into Healthy Habits

Professional endurance racer, Phil Hanson, told me in an interview that some of the behaviors that started from his fitness goals become habits for life, whether the goal is in place or not. He explained:

> *"The fact that I'm trying to lose weight while not losing lean muscle meant that I was having a high-protein diet. So I started having my first meal of the day being a lean protein shake. But I've been doing that now for five months, even though I haven't had the weight loss goal for the entire five months. It started as a goal but has transitioned into a habit that has stayed with me and will likely stay with me because it provides me with an advantage. I understand the reason behind it, and I don't see any negatives associated with it."*

The North Star Approach

I'm now fifty-six years old, and at this wise old age, I rarely use goals the way I've described them in this book. Don't get me wrong, I'm still striving, and most people looking at my life from the outside might think I'm still incredibly achievement oriented. After all:

- I still want to grow my business to a value of $100 million
- I still want a health span of 100 years (notice I didn't say lifespan)
- I still want my emotional connections with my family to get stronger year after year
- I still want to write 100 books before I die

Yet, these are not traditional goals to me anymore. Instead, they represent my North Stars.

As Ralph Waldo Emerson once said, "It's not the destination. It's the journey." This philosophy is reminiscent of ancient travelers who navigated vast terrains and treacherous seas using the North Star. This star, the brightest in the Little Dipper constellation, remains constant due to its alignment with the Earth's axis while other stars appear to move around it.

The North Star doesn't signify a destination but guides the path, offering the right direction even amid meandering journeys. I may or may not build a $100 million business or enjoy robust health until 100, but striving toward these North Stars undeniably enriches my daily life.

Parallel to this, I emphasize daily habits over goals. Habits are about the continuous journey of improvement, not about a fixed endpoint. They align with the present, where true, enduring transformation takes place.

Each morning I reflect on my "Three to Thrive" North Stars. And for each, I ask myself, "What will I do today, to make that tomorrow a reality?" I then rehearse my day. For health, I'll think about what I'm going to eat and when. When I'll stretch, lift, and get my 10,000 steps in. When I'll meditate.

By developing daily habits in our North Star areas, there is indeed progress, and there will be notable gains, but the focus is no longer on the gap that remains.

QUOTE

*"We are what we repeatedly do. Excellence, then, is not an act but a habit." –**Will Durant***

The Final Secret

It's all about the journey.

The 'Impossible to Inevitable' Goal Setting Assessment

This self-assessment is based on 10 science-based secrets to effective goal setting. Answer Yes or No to the questions below and reflect on the strategies you may or may not be using to maximize goal effectiveness.

1. I strongly believe that setting goals can significantly improve my performance in various aspects of my life. (Yes / No)

2. I maintain strong focus and perseverance when pursuing a goal, even when faced with challenges and setbacks. (Yes / No)

3. I am comfortable setting goals that are ambitious and challenging, but also attainable with effort and time. (Yes / No)

4. I set goals that are specific and measurable, so that I can clearly define what success looks like. (Yes / No)

5. I regularly monitor my progress against my goals, using milestones, metrics, and feedback to make adjustments as needed. (Yes / No)

6. I am highly committed to my goals, even when I encounter obstacles, distractions, or competing priorities. (Yes / No)

7. I actively seek out new knowledge, skills, or resources that can help me achieve my goals more effectively and efficiently. (Yes / No)

8. I intentionally create an environment that supports my goals, such as removing distractions, seeking support from others, or using tools and systems to streamline my workflow. (Yes / No)

9. I rarely procrastinate and manage my time and energy well to stay on track towards my goals. (Yes / No)

10. I prioritize balancing my pursuit of goals with other aspects of my life, such as relationships, health, and leisure activities, to maintain overall well-being and fulfillment. (Yes / No)

INTERPRETING RESULTS

If your total number of YES answers is less than 5, you should reread this book and focus on improving your goal setting strategies before setting new goals.

If your total number of YES answers is 6 to 8, you are practicing good goal strategies, and have room for improvement.

If your total number of YES answers is 9 to 10, you have achieved a high level of goal setting mastery.

LIVE SPEECH

Hire Kevin to Speak

Kevin Kruse speaks around the world at annual conferences, executive retreats, and sales meetings. Based on his bestselling book, 11 Secrets Successful People Know About Goal setting, Kevin shares the surprising science-backed ways people can achieve anything—without delay, derailing, or procrastination.

To invite Kevin to speak at your next event, email info@kevinkruse.com or call 267-702-6760.

ABOUT THE AUTHOR

Kevin Kruse

Kevin Kruse is a *New York Times* bestselling author, *Forbes* contributor, and founder of several multi-million-dollar companies. He has advised *Fortune* 500 CEOs, Marine Corps officers, and members of Congress. He currently serves as Founder + CEO of LEADx, with the mission to spark the next 100 million leaders around the world.

In pursuit of the American Dream, Kevin started his first company when he was just 22 years old. He worked around the clock, living out of his one-room office and showering each day at the local YMCA, before giving up a year later deeply in debt. But after discovering the secrets of the most successful entrepreneurs, athletes, leaders, and parents, Kevin went on to build and sell several successful companies, winning *Inc.* 500 and Best Place to Work awards along the way.

Website: www.KevinKruse.com
LinkedIn: www.linkedin.com/in/kevinkruse67/
Twitter: @kruse
Instagram: @kevinauthor

**To invite Kevin to speak at your next event,
email info@kevinkruse.com or call 267-702-6760.**

ALSO FROM KEVIN KRUSE

Double Your Productivity
Without Feeling Overworked or Overwhelmed

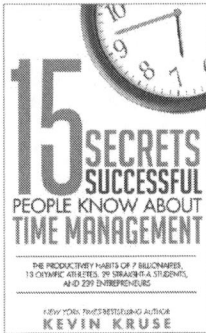

What if a few new habits could dramatically increase your productivity, and even 5x or 10x it in key areas?

Based on survey research and interviews with billionaires, Olympic athletes, straight-A students, and over 200 entrepreneurs—-including Mark Cuban, Kevin Harrington, James Altucher, John Lee Dumas, Pat Flynn, Grant Cardone, and Lewis Howes—-Kruse answers the question: what are the secrets to extreme productivity? In this book, you'll learn:

- Why millionaires don't use to-do lists (and what they DO use)
- How to cure procrastination with the "Time Travel" trick
- How the Harvard "DDR Questions" save 8 hours a week
- How to identify your REAL priorities
- How to get to zero emails in your inbox using 321Zero
- How the simple E-3C system will double your productivity
- How to reduce stress with the Richard Branson Tool
- How to leave work at 5:00 without feeling guilty
- How to run meetings like Apple, Google & Virgin
- How to conquer social media distractions

Why Great Leaders Make No Rules, Close Their Open Door, Crowd Their Calendar, Play Favorites, and Lead with Love

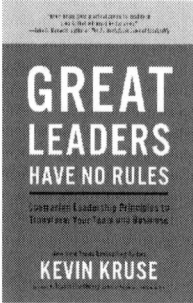

Be the boss everyone wants to work for and the high achiever every company wants to hire—all without drama, stress, or endless hours in the office.

You will learn:

- Why you need to close your open-door policy (and what to replace it with)
- How rules destroy culture and families (and what to do instead)
- Why you should strive to be likable (but not necessarily liked)
- How to lead with love (even if you don't like them)
- Why you should play favorites with team members

Build Your Personal Brand
In Just An Hour A Day

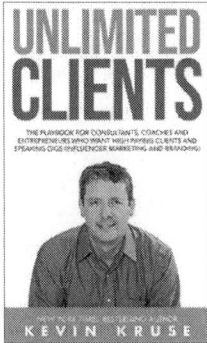

Do you want to BUILD YOUR PERSONAL BRAND as a coach, consultant, author, creative artist, small business owner or entrepreneur?

Based on his own success as an Inc 500 entrepreneur and New York Times bestselling author and global speaker, Kevin Kruse reveals how to:

- Become a go-to Thought Leader in less than a year
- Quickly build your audience using other people's Facebook groups with the Visiting-Sherpa Strategy
- Turn newsletter subscribers into "Superfans" who buy everything you release with the Ben Franklin Effect (repeat this every week)
- Generate sales from even the smallest email list with the Intimate Attention Secret
- Discover your subscribers' true interests and needs with the Reply-Challenge Technique
- Learn the secret to making an impact and creating a life that truly matters

Made in United States
Troutdale, OR
02/02/2025